RETURN *to the* COMMON GRILL

Return *to the* Common Grill

Chef Craig Common

Huron River Press
201 South Main Street, Suite 900
Ann Arbor, MI 48104
www.huronriverpress.com

Photography: Mark Thomas, Grand Rapids, Michigan
Photography Assistant: Bob Hazen
Food Stylist: Loretta Gorman
Book Design: Savitski Design, Ann Arbor, Michigan

Printed and bound in China

10 9 8 7 6 5 4 3 2 1

Library of Congress Cataloging-in-Publication Data

Common, Craig.
    Return to the Common Grill / Craig Common.
        p. cm.
    ISBN 1-932399-09-7
    1. Cookery. 2. Common Grill (Restaurant) I. Common Grill
(Restaurant) II. Title.
    TX714.C637 2005
    641.5--dc22
                            2005019555

Dedication "To My Family: My wife Donna for never-end-
ing support, my daughter Rachel for providing music in my
life, and my son Brett for inspiring me to be a better golfer…"

Acknowledgements

To Ann B. for being my fitness guru.
To Rochelle for editing and helping with this project.
To Mike Savitski for your work putting this book together.
To Mark Thomas and his crew for your wonderful photography.
To Shira Klein of Huron River Press for her care and dedication.
To Kate, Kathy, Justin, Sean, Kari, and Carrie for your hard work putting together the recipes to be photographed.

Extended Dedication/Acknowledgement:

To Bob, Jack, Gil, Paul, Dudley, Mark, George, Larry and Del for allowing me the opportunity to succeed as owner of my own restaurant. I am forever grateful for your confidence in my abilities.

To Joe and Tom for being the best buddies one could have.

To Patti Kucera — the absolute best manager in the world. She has been with us since the restaurant started and she truly understands what hospitality is all about. I am indebted to her for her continued dedication.

To my present managers for their continued dedication and hard work.

To my suppliers throughout the years, for providing The Grill with great products so we can continue to provide our guests with the best.

To all past employees who have gone to be successful in their careers after spending time here at The Grill. I have always hoped that their time at The Grill had a positive impact on their careers and that, once they moved on, they would be the cream of the crop in their business or academic pursuits. With that in mind, my hats off to all the restauranteurs, caterers, doctors, nurses, teachers, managers and chefs who spent time at The Grill. Keep striving to be the best. I'm proud of all of you.

To the most important part of The Grill — our guests. We have been incredibly blessed to have a loyal following who continue to trust us year after year to provide them with quality food, service, and the comfort of knowing that their needs will be anticipated and met. We take pride in the fact that our guests are our top priority. We thank all of you for your incredible support!

And finally, to our greatest asset, my staff. Without their commitment The Grill would be just another restaurant. We have been blessed with a staff who, for many years, has believed in our philosophy of hospitality. We have many people that have been with us for more than 10 years and it makes for a great environment. It has been a wonderful opportunity, throughout the years, to watch my own family grow alongside that of my employees. My sincere gratitude to all current and past employees for carrying on The Common Grill tradition!

"...and to my mom who inspired it all." — Craig Common

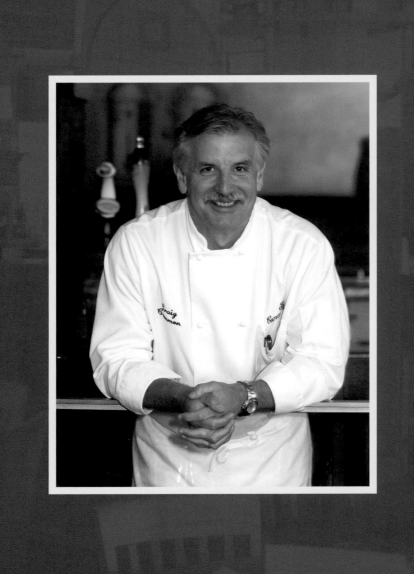

Introduction

It hardly seems possible that 14 years have passed since we first opened our doors. When I think back, it feels like only yesterday that I was standing in front of my new employees, asking them to trust in me and the journey that we were about to begin. Who could have guessed, that 14 years later, The Common Grill could experience so much success?

It's a privilege to have worked with so many people over the years, but I'm especially honored and proud that many of our employees have been with us since opening day. It's also an honor to know, that over the years, many of our past employees have gone on to become loyal guests. The sense of pride and ownership present amongst both past and present employees makes not only for a great workplace, but it helps make us feel more like family. Without them, the restaurant would not be a success.

In the past 14 years, with the success of the restaurant, I have been given some incredible opportunities. In 1997, I had the privilege of being invited to cook at the James Beard House in New York — an incredible experience which I will never forget. In 2002, we were honored to be included in *Bon Appetit's* Best Neighborhood Restaurants in the Midwest article. And, of course, a highlight of past summers has been my involvement in the Michigan Chef's Dinner in Northern Michigan at Tapawingo, working with some of Michigan's finest chefs. Tapawingo is one of my favorite restaurants in the country. It is always great to work with Pete Peterson and his staff.

But, the highlight of my career was in 2000 when the first Common Grill cookbook was released and we received such an overwhelmingly positive response. At the time, I was sure it was a once in a lifetime experience. So, when Huron River Press approached me for a second cookbook, I knew it was something I had to do.

I'm very excited to be sharing new recipes with you for a second time. We specialize in seafood at The Common Grill and, with that in mind I've included quite a few seafood recipes. I hope this cookbook challenges you to get creative in the kitchen and experience different tastes but, most of all, I hope you have fun.

Enjoy!

These sauces, oils and
stocks will improve the
flavor of your food and
have you prepared to make
many of the recipes in this
book. You can freeze most
of them into smaller por-
tions and be ready to roll
with the recipes!

The Essentials

Olive Oil, Garlic & Herb Sauce

2½	cups **olive oil**
6	cloves roasted **garlic**
3	tablespoons **Seafood Base** (see sources, page 192)
1	cup hot **water**
2	tablespoons fresh **parsley**, finely chopped
2	**sun-dried tomatoes**, finely chopped

Place 1 cup of olive oil in food processor with garlic. Process until garlic is thoroughly blended. Set aside.

In small bowl, mix Seafood Base with ½ cup of hot water. Stir until completely dissolved. Set aside.

Place remaining olive oil in saucepan and heat until just below boiling point.

Add garlic and oil mixture and immediately remove from heat. Mix well. Stir in parsley and sun dried tomatoes. Add Seafood Base mixture and remaining ½ cup hot water. Whisk entire mixture until thoroughly combined. Refrigerate.

Makes 3½ cups

Roasted Garlic Butter

1	cup **butter**, softened
1	clove roasted **garlic**
¼	cup **dry white wine**
2	teaspoons fresh **parsley**, finely chopped
1	tablespoon roasted **yellow pepper**, finely chopped
1	tablespoon roasted **red pepper**, finely chopped
½	teaspoon **kosher salt**
¼	teaspoon cracked **black pepper**

Place softened butter in mixer and whip well. Set aside.

In food processor, blend garlic, wine and parsley until thoroughly mixed.

Add remaining ingredients and the whipped butter and mix well.

Refrigerate until ready to use.

Makes 1½ cups

Tomato Basil Sauce

2	tablespoons **olive oil**
2	cloves **garlic**, finely chopped
1	small **onion**, finely chopped
2	teaspoons fresh **basil**, finely chopped
2	teaspoons fresh **oregano**, finely chopped
1	tablespoon fresh **parsley**, finely chopped
1¼	cups **dry white wine**
1	28 oz. can crushed **tomatoes**
1	tablespoon **Seafood Base** (see sources, page 192)

Heat oil in small pot and add garlic.

Add onions and sauté in the hot oil until soft.

Add basil and oregano and cook for one minute.

Add parsley and mix well.

Add wine, tomatoes, and Seafood Base. Mix well.
Bring to a boil and continue cooking for 10 minutes.

Remove from stove.

Refrigerate until ready to use.

Makes 4 cups

Tomato Concasse

1	large **red tomato**, seeded, diced small
1	large **yellow tomato**, seeded, diced small
2	tablespoons **extra virgin olive oil**
¼	teaspoon **black pepper**
1	teaspoon **kosher salt**
1	tablespoon fresh **chives**, chopped

Combine all ingredients in mixing bowl.

Refrigerate until ready to use.

Makes 1 cup

Red Bell Pepper Butter

1	lb. **butter**, softened
2	tablespoons **butter**, melted
2	**red bell peppers**, roasted, seeded, skins removed
4	cloves **garlic**
1	**green onion**, coarsely chopped
1	teaspoon fresh **parsley**, finely chopped
½	teaspoon **cayenne pepper**
½	teaspoon fresh **thyme**, finely chopped

Place softened butter in bowl and beat until very fluffy. Set aside.

Place red peppers, melted butter, garlic, and onion in food processor. Purée.

Transfer to softened butter mixture; add chopped parsley, cayenne pepper, and thyme and mix thoroughly.

Refrigerate until ready to use.

Makes 1 lb.

Chicken Stock

3	quarts **water**
5	lbs. **chicken bones**
1	**onion**, diced
2	ribs **celery**, diced
2	**carrots**, diced
1	**leek**, thoroughly cleaned and diced
1	tablespoon **kosher salt**
2	cloves **garlic**, diced
1	tablespoon cracked **black pepper**
4	fresh **basil** leaves
4	fresh **parsley** sprigs
4	fresh **thyme** sprigs

Place all ingredients in a large stockpot. Cover and bring to a boil. Reduce heat and simmer for 2 hours. Remove chicken bones and strain.

Refrigerate until ready to use.

Makes 2 quarts

Brown Chicken Stock

3	lbs. **chicken bones**
2	tablespoons **olive oil**
1	cup **red onions**, thinly sliced
1	rib **celery**, chopped
1	cup **carrots**, chopped
8	cups **water**
1	**garlic bulb**, cut in half
1	sprig fresh **thyme**
1	sprig fresh **parsley**
1	sprig fresh **basil**
½	teaspoon **kosher salt**
¼	teaspoon cracked **black pepper**

Preheat oven to 450°.

Roast chicken bones for 1 hour or until browned (after 30 minutes remove from oven and discard any fat. Return to oven for remaining 30 minutes).

Heat oil in stockpot over medium heat, add onions, celery and carrots, and cook until golden. Reduce heat and cook for 10 minutes until well browned.

Transfer chicken bones to stock pot and add enough water to cover bones by 2".

Bring to a boil. Add garlic, thyme, parsley, basil, salt and black pepper. Reduce heat to low and cook for 2 hours. Add water when needed.

Strain. Transfer to a clean pot. Simmer over low heat for an additional hour. Remove from heat and strain again.

Refrigerate until ready to use.

Makes 2 quarts

Fish Stock

2½	lbs. **fish bones**
⅔	cup **Spanish onions**, thinly sliced
8	sprigs fresh **parsley**
3	sprigs fresh **thyme**
2	fresh **basil** leaves
1	quart **water**
1	cup **white wine**

Place all ingredients in large stockpot and bring to a slow boil.

Reduce heat and simmer for 30 minutes.

Remove from heat and allow to rest for 15 minutes. Strain.

Refrigerate until ready to use.

Makes 4 cups

Beef Stock

2½	lbs.	**beef short rib bones**
1	tablespoon	**olive oil**
2	tablespoons	**tomato paste**
½	cup	**Spanish onions**, chopped
¼	cup	**carrots**, chopped
¼	cup	**celery**, chopped
1	head	**garlic**, halved
8	cups	**water**
1	fresh	**thyme** sprig
1	fresh	**oregano** sprig
1	fresh	**parsley** sprig
1	teaspoon	**kosher salt**
2	fresh	**basil** leaves

Preheat oven to 450°.

Place short rib bones in an ovenproof pan. Drizzle olive oil over bones. Bake in oven for 30 minutes, or until bones are browned.

Transfer bones to stockpot. Add tomato paste, onions, carrots, celery, garlic, thyme, oregano, parsley, salt and basil.

Add cold water and bring to a boil. When water boils, reduce heat and simmer for 2 hours.

Remove from heat and strain.

Refrigerate until ready to use.

Makes 4 cups

Lobster Stock

2½	lbs.	**Lobster Purée*** or **Lobster Shells**
⅔	cup	**Spanish onions**, thinly sliced
8	fresh	**parsley** sprigs
3	fresh	**thyme** sprigs
2	fresh	**basil** leaves
1		**garlic** clove, chopped
4	cups	**tomato paste**
1	quart	**water**
1	cup	**white wine**

Place all ingredients in a large stockpot and bring to a slow boil.

Reduce heat and simmer for 45 minutes. Remove from heat and let rest for 15 minutes.

Strain well.

Refrigerate until ready to use.

Most fish markets carry Lobster Purée.

Makes 4 cups

Lamb Jus

1	lb. **lamb bones**
1	small **onion**, chopped
1	**carrot**, chopped
4	**mushrooms**, chopped
1	rib **celery**, chopped
1	**garlic bulb**, cut in half
1	tablespoon **tomato paste**
2	**basil** leaves
¼	teaspoon cracked **black pepper**
2	tablespoons **red wine**
1	tablespoon **olive oil**

Preheat oven to 400°.

Arrange lamb bones in roasting pan and drizzle olive oil over top.

Add vegetables and cook until brown.

Deglaze pan with red wine. Transfer to stockpot and add remainder of ingredients.

Add enough water to cover bones by 2".

Bring to a boil and then simmer for 3 hours.

Remove from heat and strain.

Refrigerate until ready to use.

Makes 4 cups

Vegetable Stock

¼	cup **olive oil**
2	small **red onions**, quartered
2	ribs **celery**
1	**leek**, split and washed
2	**carrots**, peeled, coarsely chopped
4	**tomatoes**, chopped in large pieces
4	fresh **parsley** sprigs
4	fresh **thyme** sprigs
4	**basil** leaves
2	**garlic** cloves
½	teaspoon **kosher salt**
½	teaspoon **Peppercorn Melange Mix**
4	quarts **water**

Heat oil in stockpot on medium high heat.

Add onions, celery, leeks and carrots and cook until soft.

Add tomatoes, herbs, garlic, salt and Peppercorn Melange Mix. Stir together.

Add 4 quarts water and bring to a boil.

Reduce heat and simmer for 1 hour.

Remove from stove and strain.

Refrigerate until ready to use.

Makes 3 quarts

Veal Jus

5	lbs.	**veal bones**
2	tablespoons	**olive oil**
2	tablespoons	**tomato paste**
1	small	**Spanish onion**
2	large	**carrots**, chopped
1		**garlic bulb**, halved
2	ribs	**celery**, chopped
4	fresh	**thyme** springs
4	fresh	**oregano** sprigs
4	fresh	**parsley** sprigs
8	fresh	**basil** leaves
1	teaspoon	**kosher salt**
2	quarts	**water**
1	quart	**dry red wine**

Preheat oven to 450°.

Place veal bones in large roasting pan. Drizzle with olive oil. Place in oven and brown for 30 minutes.

Remove from roasting pan and place in stockpot with tomato paste, onions, carrots, garlic, celery, herbs and kosher salt.

Add cold water and dry red wine and place on stove. Bring to a boil, then reduce heat and simmer for 4 hours.

Remove from stove and strain.

Refrigerate until ready to use.

Makes 2 quarts

Ginger Cilantro Batter

2	cups	**rice flour**
2	cups	**water**
2	tablespoons	**ginger**, grated
2	tablespoons	**cilantro**, finely chopped

Combine all ingredients in mixing bowl.

Refrigerate until ready to use.

This is what we use for our soft shell crabs when in season, but this batter is also great on shrimp or fish.

Makes 4 cups

Foccacia Bread Dough

2   cups warm **water** (100°)
2   packages **yeast** (1¼ oz. each dry yeast)
4   teaspoons **sugar**
1   tablespoon **kosher salt**
4   tablespoons **olive oil**
6   cups **High Gluten flour**

Mix warm water, yeast, sugar, salt, and olive oil together to dissolve yeast in mixer bowl.

Add flour and mix about 5 minutes or until dough is of a smooth consistency.

Remove from mixer and divide into 4 portions. Brush with oil to retain moisture.

Shape each one in long shaped piece.

Place them on a cookie sheet and set under refrigeration until needed to be shaped for foccacia.

Makes 24 pieces

Kosher Salt / Poppy Seed Foccacia Bread

1   lb. **Foccacia Bread Dough** (1 portion; see recipe this page)
2   tablespoons **Herb Marinade** (see page 22)
1   tablespoon **Focaccia Topping** (see recipe below)

Foccacia Topping
4   tablespoons **kosher salt**
2   tablespoons **poppy seeds**

For Foccacia Topping   Mix together.

Preheat oven to 350°.

Roll dough out to fit 6 x 8-inch baking pan and place in pan.

Sprinkle with Foccacia Topping.

Drizzle Herb Marinade over top of dough.

Allow to rise ¾".

Place in preheated oven until golden in color (about 25 minutes). Allow to cool.

Cut into 6 squares.

High Gluten flour is Bread flour.

Herb Marinade

4	cloves **garlic**
1	cup **olive oil**
1	tablespoon fresh **basil**, finely chopped
1	tablespoon fresh **oregano**, finely chopped

Place ½ cup of the olive oil and all of the garlic in the food processor and blend well.

Add remaining ½ cup of the olive oil, basil and oregano and mix well.

Refrigerate until ready to use.

Makes 1 cup

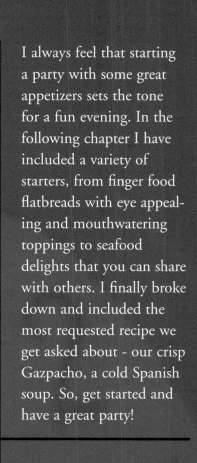

I always feel that starting a party with some great appetizers sets the tone for a fun evening. In the following chapter I have included a variety of starters, from finger food flatbreads with eye appealing and mouthwatering toppings to seafood delights that you can share with others. I finally broke down and included the most requested recipe we get asked about - our crisp Gazpacho, a cold Spanish soup. So, get started and have a great party!

Appetizers

Gazpacho

1   tablespoon **garlic**, emulsify with oil

1   28 oz. can **crushed tomatoes**

1   cup seedless **cucumbers**, peeled,
       finely chopped

½   cup **green peppers**, core removed,
       finely chopped

1   cup **onions**, finely chopped

2   tablespoons **red pepper**,
       finely chopped

1   tablespoon fresh **parsley**,
       finely chopped

      pinch of **salt**

      pinch of **pepper**

½   cup **Wishbone Italian Dressing**

1¼   cups **tomato juice**

Garnish for each serving

1   **cucumber** slice, sliced thick on bias

6   **croutons**, freshly made

1   sprig **watercress**

1   teaspoon **sour cream**

Place garlic into blender along with a little of the oil from the top of the Wishbone Italian Dressing. Blend well.

Add remaining ingredients and mix well. Refrigerate and allow to chill for about 2 hours.

Place gazpacho into serving bowl.

Place cucumber slice on side of bowl.

Place sour cream in center of gazpacho.

Lay croutons on top of soup and garnish with watercress.

This is a great recipe to use on warm summer nights. It is truly refreshing.

Chilled Mussels Diablo

½	cup **olive oil**
2	**jalapeño peppers**, sliced ⅛"
2	cloves **garlic**, smashed
2	2 lb. package **mussels** (100 pre-cleaned)
1	cup **sherry wine**
¼	teaspoon **dry mustard**
1	teaspoon fresh **chives**, chopped

Heat oil in large sauté pan.

Sauté jalapeños for about 1 minute. Be careful not to burn.

Add garlic and cook until golden.

Immediately add mussels, sherry and dry mustard. Shake pan well. Cover and cook for 2 minutes.

Remove cover, flip mussels. Cover again and keep cooking until all the mussels are open. This will take about 5 minutes.

Remove from heat and keep under refrigeration until ready to serve.

Place mussels on large serving platter or 6 individual plates.

Pour broth over mussels.

Top with chopped chives.

Suggested Wine: Chappellet Chenin Blanc 2002 Napa Valley

Creole BBQ Shrimp

20	pieces large **shrimp**, deveined, tail on
1	cup **Creole BBQ Sauce** (see recipe below)
2	tablespoons **Roasted Garlic Butter** (see page 14)
2	cups **Pecan Wild Rice Pilaf** (see page 140)
4	teaspoons fresh **chives**, finely chopped

Creole BBQ Sauce

½	teaspoon **cayenne pepper**
½	teaspoon **black pepper**
¼	teaspoon **salt**
¼	teaspoon **red pepper flakes**
2	sprigs fresh **thyme**
2	sprigs fresh **rosemary**
2	sprigs fresh **oregano**
1	clove **garlic**, finely chopped
½	teaspoon **Lea & Perrins**
¼	cup **dark beer**
2	tablespoons **Roasted Garlic Butter**, melted (see page 14)
½	cup **clam juice**
1	teaspoon **Creole mustard**

For Creole BBQ Sauce Combine all ingredients in a mixing bowl. Blend well with wire whisk.

Refrigerate until ready to use.

Preparation Place Creole BBQ Sauce and shrimp into sauté pan and cook over high heat until shrimp are cooked.

Place ½ cup Pecan Wild Rice in center of each serving platter. Remove shrimp from sauce and divide equally in a circle around the rice with the tails pointing in towards the rice for a nice presentation.

Return pan to heat and add 2 tablespoons Roasted Garlic Butter. Stir well until melted.

Remove pan from stove and pour sauce evenly over shrimp and rice.

Sprinkle chopped chives over both shrimp and rice.

Suggested Wine: Cline Zinfandel 2002 California

Fried Spicy Smelt

2   lbs. **smelt**
     Spicy Breading for dusting
        (see recipe below)
     Red Pepper-Garlic Mayonnaise
        (see recipe below)
6   **lemon wedges**

Spicy Breading
2   cups **Drake's Fry Crisp Batter Mix**
3   tablespoons **Paul Prudhomme's
     Cajun Spice Mix**

Red Pepper-Garlic Mayonnaise
(Makes 1 cup)
⅔   cup **mayonnaise**
¼   teaspoon **dry mustard**
⅛   teaspoon **cayenne pepper**
¼   cup **Red Bell Pepper Butter**, melted
        (see page 16)
1   tablespoon **Roasted Garlic Butter**,
        melted (see page 14)

Preparation Dust smelt in Spicy Breading and deep fry until crisp.

Place on serving plate.

Serve with lemon wedge and Red Pepper-Garlic Mayonnaise.

For Spicy Breading Mix all ingredients together. Store in a dry place until ready to use.

For Red Pepper-Garlic Mayonnaise In medium bowl, using wire whisk, beat together mayonnaise, dry mustard, and cayenne pepper.

Add Red Bell Pepper Butter and beat until creamy.

Mix in Roasted Garlic Butter.

This is a great Midwest treat. Ask your seafood market to order these and have fun watching the reaction of your guests when you serve them as an appetizer.

28   Appetizers   Return to the Common Grill

Mussels Marinara

2	2 lb. packages **mussels** (100 pre-cleaned)
½	cup **white wine**
½	cup **Roasted Garlic Butter** (see page 14)
½	cup **Tomato Basil Sauce** (see page 15)
½	cup **water**
2	**shallots**, sliced thinly
2	**jalapeño peppers**, finely chopped
1	cup cooked **pancetta**, julienned
6	pieces grilled **garlic bread**
6	teaspoons fresh **chives**, chopped

Place mussels, white wine, Roasted Garlic Butter, Tomato Basil Sauce, water, shallots, jalapeño pepper and pancetta into a sauté pan.

Cover and cook over medium heat until mussels have opened.

Pour into serving dish.

Top with chopped chives and grilled garlic bread.

Suggested Wine: Château St. Jean Fume Blanc 2001 Sonoma

Steamed Red Curry Mussels

2   2 lb. packages **mussels**,
       (100 pre-cleaned)

3   cups **Red Curry Sauce**
       (see recipe below)

6   tablespoons **Tomato Concasse**
       (see page 15)

6   teaspoons fresh **chives**, chopped

Red Curry Sauce *(Makes 1 quart)*

2   tablespoons **butter**
2   tablespoons **peanut oil**
2   teaspoons **garlic**, finely chopped
2   tablespoons **ginger**
1   teaspoon **ground cumin**
1   teaspoon **curry powder**
1   teaspoon **paprika**
4   tablespoons **crushed tomatoes**
2   tablespoons **red curry paste**
3   cups unsweetened **coconut milk**
2   teaspoons **cilantro**, finely chopped

Place mussels and Red Curry Sauce into sauté pan and cover. Cook until mussels have opened.

Pour into serving dish.

Place Tomato Concasse on top and sprinkle with chopped chives.

For Red Curry Sauce Heat butter and oil in saucepan.

Sauté garlic and ginger for 2 minutes until soft.

Add cumin, curry powder, paprika and crushed tomatoes.

Sauté for 2–3 minutes.

Add curry paste and coconut milk and stir until paste dissolves.

Add chopped cilantro and mix well.

Suggested Wine: Geyser Peak Chardonnay 2001 Ricci Vineyard

Seared Ahi Tuna

4	4 oz. pieces **ahi tuna**, 2" x 2"
½	cup **Kikkoman Teriyaki Sauce**
8	teaspoons **five-spice powder**, for dusting tuna
½	cup **Wakame Seaweed Salad***
½	cup **Soy Mustard Dipping Sauce** (see page 182)
4	teaspoons fresh **chives**, chopped

Marinate tuna in Kikkoman Teriyaki sauce for 1 hour.

Dust tuna with five-spice powder.

Place tuna into hot sauté pan and sear tuna on all sides until rare. Remove from pan and slice thinly.

Place seaweed salad in center of serving platter.

Place sliced tuna around seaweed salad and serve with Soy Mustard Dipping Sauce.

Garnish with chopped chives.

*Wakame Seaweed Salad is available at most seafood markets.

Suggested Wine: Coppola Diamond Series, Chardonnay 2002 California

Portabella Wellington

4   3" **portabella mushroom caps**

½   cup **Herb Marinade**
          (see page 22)

4   pieces **puff pastry**, ¼" thick,
          4" x 4" pieces

4   tablespoons **Rosemary Port Butter**,
          softened (see recipe below)

4   tablespoons **Roquefort cheese**,
          crumbled

2   teaspoons fresh **chives**, chopped

Egg-Cream Wash

2   **eggs**

¼   cup **cream**

Rosemary Port Butter *(Makes 1 cup)*

1   cup **port wine**

3   **shallots**, thinly sliced

1   tablespoon **rice wine vinegar**

¼   teaspoon cracked **black pepper**

4   sprigs fresh **rosemary**

½   teaspoon **pomegranate molasses**
          (see sources, page 192)

⅛   teaspoon **dry mustard**

½   cup **butter**, softened

½   teaspoon **Dijon mustard**

¼   teaspoon **kosher salt**

Preparation Preheat oven to 350°.

Marinate portabella mushrooms in Herb Marinade for one hour.

Roast mushrooms in oven until soft, about 10 minutes. Allow to cool.

Cut puff pastry sheet into 4" x 4" pieces. This will encase mushroom.

Place softened 1 tablespoon Rosemary Port Butter on top of each mushroom cap. Place 1 tablespoon crumbled Roquefort on top of Rosemary Port Butter. Place puff pastry over top of mushroom and tuck pastry underneath cap.

Brush with Egg-Cream Wash.

Refrigerate until ready to use.

Service Preparation Preheat oven to 400°.

Place mushroom in oven and cook until pastry is golden, about 20 minutes.

Pour excess sauce onto serving plate and place mushroom on top. Garnish with chopped chives.

This is my spin on an appetizer that I had at the "Fifth Floor Restaurant" in San Francisco. I thought it was very clever and excellent at the same time.

For Egg-Cream Wash Whisk together.

For Rosemary Port Butter Combine wine, shallots, vinegar, pepper, herbs, pomegranate molasses and dry mustard in a saucepan and boil over medium heat until liquid is syrup, about 15–20 minutes. Strain and allow to cool.

Combine with butter, Dijon mustard and salt.

Refrigerate until ready to use.

Suggested Wine: Foley Santa Maria Hills Pinot Noir 2001 California

Cured Smoked Salmon *with* Corn Cakes

18   slices **smoked salmon**
          (approximately 1 lb.)
12   **Poblano-Corn Cakes**
          (see page 35)
6   tablespoons **Jalapeño Crème
          Fraîche** (see opposite page)
6   teaspoons **Herb Garniture**
          (see recipe below)
6   teaspoons **butter**, melted

Herb Garniture
1   tablespoon fresh **dill**,
          finely chopped
1   tablespoon fresh **chives**,
          finely chopped
2   teaspoons **shallots**, rinsed, dried
          and finely chopped
2   teaspoons **capers**, whole

Preparation Brush Poblano Corn Potato Cakes with melted butter and place under broiler in oven. Cook until hot and golden.

Place 2 cakes on each serving platter on one side stacked in fan fashion.

Roll 3 slices of cured salmon and place on top of Poblano Corn Cakes.

Sprinkle 1 teaspoon Herb Garniture over top of salmon.

Drizzle 1 tablespoon Jalapeño Crème Fraîche over top of salmon and Poblano Corn Cakes.

For Herb Garniture Mix together and refrigerate until ready to use.

Suggested Wine: Lockwood Chardonnay 2002 Monterey

Poblano-Corn Cakes

⅔ cup **yellow corn flour (Masa Harina)**
⅓ cup **all-purpose flour**
½ teaspoon **baking powder**
¼ teaspoon **baking soda**
2 teaspoons **sugar**
½ teaspoon **salt**
⅓ cup **buttermilk**
1 **egg**, beaten
1 cup **Roasted Corn Poblano Relish**
   (see recipe below)

Roasted Corn-Poblano Relish
(Makes 2 cups)
2 **ears fresh corn**, grilled
2 tablespoons **butter**, melted
1 **Poblano chili pepper**, grilled
4 tablespoons **red pepper**,
   finely chopped
¼ cup **green onion**, sliced thin
¼ cup **red onion**, finely chopped
2 tablespoons **cilantro**, finely chopped
1 tablespoon **lime juice**
2 teaspoons **olive oil**
1 **garlic** clove, finely chopped
¼ cup **beefsteak tomato**, chopped
   into ½" pieces

Jalapeño Crème Fraîche *(Makes 2 cups)*
⅓ cup **Crème Fraîche**
1 **jalapeño pepper**, seeded,
   finely chopped
1 tablespoon **cilantro**, finely chopped
   pinch **white pepper**
¼ teaspoon fresh **lemon juice**
¼ teaspoon **Tabasco Sauce**

Preparation Mix flours, baking powder, baking soda, sugar and salt in a mixing bowl.

Add eggs and buttermilk to dry ingredients and mix well.

Add Roasted Corn Poblano Relish and mix well.

Allow to rest for 15 minutes before cooking on griddle.

Using a quarter cup measure, place cakes on griddle and cook at 350° until cakes are golden on both sides.

Place on cookie sheet and cover with plastic wrap until ready to use.

For Roasted Corn-Poblano Relish Brush corn with butter and place on grill. Turn corn to grill on all sides. Set aside until ready to take off cob.

Place Poblano pepper on grill and char on all sides.

Seed and chop Poblano pepper into ¼" pieces.

Take corn off the cob and place in mixing bowl. Combine with all other ingredients and mix well.

For Jalapeño Crème Fraîche Add all ingredients to a food processor and purée until smooth.

Keep at room temperature.

Grilled Scallops *with* Mango BBQ Sauce

1	lb. **scallops**, large size
4	teaspoons **olive oil**
	salt
	paprika
1	cup **Mango BBQ Sauce** (see recipe below)
½	cup **Tomato-Red Pepper Salsa** (see page 184)
4	tablespoons **Sweet Curry Butter** (see opposite page)
4	teaspoons fresh **chives**, chopped

Mango BBQ Sauce *(Makes 4 cups)*

2	large **red tomatoes**, grilled and coarsely chopped
1	**green pepper**, grilled and coarsely chopped
1	**red pepper**, grilled and coarsely chopped
1	**mango** peeled, pitted and coarsely chopped
¼	cup **water**
¼	cup **red onions**, chopped
⅓	cup **brown sugar**
¼	cup **cider vinegar**
2	tablespoons **molasses**
2	tablespoons **Dijon mustard**
1	tablespoon **cinnamon**
1	tablespoon **garlic**, chopped
1	teaspoon **ground cumin**
1	teaspoon fresh **thyme**
1	teaspoon fresh **basil**
1	**jalapeño chili pepper**, halved

Place scallops on bamboo skewer.

Brush scallops with olive oil and sprinkle with salt and paprika.

Place on char grill at medium high heat. Cook scallops for 3–4 minutes. Turn skewer over and cook scallops until done, about 3–4 minutes. Baste scallops with Mango BBQ Sauce while cooking.

Place Tomato Red Pepper Salsa in center of serving platter.

Place scallops around salsa.

Ladle remaining Mango BBQ Sauce over top of scallops.

Drizzle scallops with Sweet Curry Butter.

Top with chopped chives.

For Mango BBQ Sauce   Combine all ingredients in large saucepot and bring to a boil.

Reduce heat and simmer for 30 minutes. Allow to cool.

Purée in food processor and refrigerate until ready to use.

Sweet Curry Butter *(Makes 2 cups)*

2	tablespoons **olive oil**
1	small **shallot**, finely chopped
1	tablespoon **curry powder**
½	teaspoon **ancho chili powder**
½	**mango**, peeled, pitted, puréed
2	tablespoons fresh **lime juice**
2	sticks **butter**, softened
½	teaspoon **kosher salt**
⅛	teaspoon **black pepper**

Tomato-Red Pepper Salsa *(Makes 2 cups)*

1	**red beefsteak tomato**, seeded, chopped into ½" pieces
1	**yellow beefsteak tomato**, seeded, chopped into ½" pieces
1	**red pepper**, chopped into ½" pieces
2	tablespoons **green onions**, finely chopped
2	tablespoons fresh **lime juice**
1	tablespoon **olive oil**
1	tablespoon **capers**, finely chopped
2	teaspoons **cilantro**, finely chopped
½	teaspoon **salt**
¼	teaspoon **black pepper**
1	**jalapeño pepper**, seeded, finely chopped
1	**garlic** clove, finely chopped

For Sweet Curry Butter Heat oil in saucepan. Add shallots and cook until soft.

Add curry powder and chile powder and continue cooking for 2–3 minutes stirring constantly.

Add mango and lime juice and cook for 5–10 more minutes on low heat.

Allow to cool.

Mix butter in mixer. Add mango mixture, salt and pepper and mix well.

Refrigerate until ready to use.

For Tomato-Red Pepper Salsa Combine all ingredients in mixing bowl.

Refrigerate until ready to use.

The Mango BBQ Sauce is fantastic on grilled salmon, swordfish or tuna. Make a batch and serve it for other dinners.

Suggested Wine: Artesa Chardonnay 2001 Carneros

Parmesan Custard *with* Wild Mushroom *and* Garlic Cream

4 portions **Parmesan Custard**
    (see recipe below)
4 portions **Wild Mushroom Skewer**
    (see recipe below)
1 cup **Garlic Cream Sauce**
    (see opposite page)
4 portions **Grilled Herb Flatbread**
    (see page 45) or **French
    Baguette grilled**
4 teaspoons fresh **chives**, chopped

Parmesan Custard
1½ cups **whipping cream**
4 **egg yolks**
1 teaspoon **unflavored gelatin**
⅓ teaspoon **Parmesan cheese**, grated
⅛ teaspoon **salt**
⅛ teaspoon **white pepper**
    pinch **nutmeg**

Wild Mushroom Skewer
Per skewer:
2 **shitake mushrooms**
2 **oyster mushrooms**
2 **chanterelle mushrooms**
1 tablespoon **Herb Marinade**
    (see opposite page)

Preparation Preheat oven to 400°.

Place Parmesan Custard in oven and cook until hot, about 5–8 minutes.

Grill Wild Mushroom Skewer on high heat and cook until soft, about 5 minutes.

Place warm Garlic Cream Sauce on serving platter.

Remove Parmesan Custard from ramekin and place on top of Garlic Cream Sauce.

Remove mushrooms from skewer and place on one side of Parmesan Custard.

Grill Herb Flatbread or French Baguette and place next to Parmesan Custard on serving platter.

Top with chopped chives.

For Parmesan Custard Preheat oven to 350°.

Bring cream to a boil. Pour into blender.

Add egg yolks, gelatin and Parmesan cheese and purée in blender.

Add salt, white pepper and nutmeg. Mix well.

Pour custard into four, ½ cup ramekins.

Place in water bath and cook in oven until set (about 60 minutes). Allow to cool.

For Wild Mushroom Skewer Preheat oven to 350°.

Place mushrooms onto bamboo skewer.

Brush with marinade and place in oven for 5 minutes to soften mushrooms.

Refrigerate until ready to use.

Fresh Herb Marinade

1	clove **garlic**, finely chopped
¼	cup **olive oil**
1	teaspoon fresh **rosemary**, finely chopped
1	teaspoon fresh **thyme**, finely chopped
1	teaspoon fresh **basil**, finely chopped
1	tablespoon **salt**
½	teaspoon **black pepper**
	juice of 1 fresh **lemon**

Garlic Cream Sauce *(Makes 2 cups)*

½	cup **Olive Oil, Garlic & Herb Sauce** (see page 14)
½	cup **Roasted Garlic Butter** (see page 14)
1	cup **heavy cream**

For Fresh Herb Marinade   Place garlic and olive oil into food processor and purée together.

Place all ingredients into mixing bowl, including emulsified garlic, and mix well.

Let stand for 1 hour before using.

For Garlic Cream Sauce   Heat Olive Oil Garlic & Herb Sauce and Roasted Garlic Butter together in large saucepan at medium heat. Cook until butter is completely melted.

Add heavy cream and cook until sauce has thickened. Remove from stove and allow to cool.

Suggested Wine: Château Julien Pinot Noir 2001 Monterey

Pan Seared Sea Scallops *with* Rock Shrimp Risotto

½   cup **olive oil**

1   lb. **sea scallops**, large size

¼   cup **leeks**, fried
     flour, for dusting leeks

1½   cups **Rock Shrimp Risotto**
     (see recipe below)

½   cup **Lobster Stock**
     (see page 18)

4   tablespoons **Basil Lemon Syrup**
     (see page 42)

4   teaspoons fresh **chives**, chopped

Rock Shrimp Risotto

½   lb. **rock shrimp**, peeled,
     deveined, tail off
     Shrimp Marinade
     (see recipe below)

⅓   cup **peanut oil**

⅔   cup **Spanish onions**, finely chopped

1½   cups **arborio rice**

⅔   cup **white wine**

2¼   cups. **Lobster Stock**
     (see page 18)

2   cups **Chicken Stock**
     (see page 16)

1   teaspoon **salt**

3   tablespoons **crushed tomatoes**

1   teaspoon **saffron**

½   teaspoon **white pepper**

3   tablespoons **butter**, chilled

3   tablespoons **Parmesan cheese**

4   tablespoons fresh **chives**, chopped

Shrimp Marinade

1   tablespoon **olive oil**

1   tablespoon fresh **chives**, chopped

3   cloves **garlic**, chopped

Place olive oil in sauté pan and heat. Add sea scallops and cook until golden on both sides, about 5–6 minutes. Remove from pan.

Dust leeks in flour and place in deep fryer and cook until crispy.

Place Rock Shrimp Risotto in sauté pan and gradually heat while mixing in Lobster Stock.

Place Rock Shrimp Risotto in center of serving platter. Place scallops around risotto.

Drizzle with Basil Lemon Syrup.

Top with fried leeks and chopped chives.

For Rock Shrimp Risotto Marinate rock shrimp for 2 hours in Shrimp Marinade.

Heat peanut oil in large saucepan.

Add onions and cook for 5-10 minutes until soft.

Add rice and continue to stir.

Deglaze with white wine and cook until liquid is absorbed.

Add 12 oz. Lobster Stock and 12 oz. Chicken Stock and cook until liquid is absorbed.

Add remaining 8 oz. Lobster Stock and 4 oz. Chicken Stock and turn on high heat.

Stir in salt, chopped tomatoes, saffron and white pepper and cook until al dente.

Add rock shrimp and cook until creamy.

Add chilled butter and Parmesan cheese and mix well.

Stir in chopped chives,

Remove from stove and refrigerate in shallow pans until ready to serve.

For Shrimp Marinade Combine all ingredients in mixing bowl.

Suggested Wine: Cuvaison Pinot Noir 2002 Carneros

Basil-Lemon Syrup

1   teaspoon **kosher salt**
1   cup fresh **basil** leaves, stems removed
        and tightly packed
½   cup **extra virgin olive oil**

Lemon Syrup
½   cup **lemon juice**
     zest from 1 **lemon**

Place salt in 1 quart water and bring to a boil.

Add basil and blanch for 30 seconds or until wilted.

Immediately plunge basil into ice water. Drain and squeeze out as much water as possible.

Place in blender with oil and blend until smooth, strain.

Add Lemon Syrup.

For Lemon Syrup In a small saucepan combine lemon juice and lemon zest and reduce to a syrup over high heat, about 5 minutes. Remove from stove and allow to cool.

Lobster-White Cheddar Quesadilla

1½ cups **Lobster-White Cheddar Quesa Mix** (see recipe below)

12 **10" flour tortillas**

3 cups **Quesa Cheese Mix** (see recipe below)

½ cup **Wesson Oil**

1½ cups **Yellow Tomato Salsa** (see page 180)

Lobster White Cheddar Mix

1 lb. **lobster meat**, chopped into ½" pieces

1 small grilled **red onion**, small dice

2 cloves **garlic**, roasted and finely chopped

1 roasted **jalapeño pepper**, seeded and finely chopped

2 tablespoons **cilantro**, finely chopped

2 teaspoons **ancho chili powder**

Quesadilla Cheese Mix

1½ cups **white cheddar cheese**, shredded

1½ cups **Monterey Jack cheese**, shredded

1 tablespoon **cilantro**, finely chopped

1 tablespoon **lemon zest**

Preparation of Quesadilla for each serving Preheat oven to 450°.

Place ¼ cup cheese on one flour tortilla.

Place ¼ cup lobster mix on top of cheese mix.

Place ¼ cup cheese mix on top of lobster mix.

Place second tortilla on top of mix and press lightly.

Brush sauté pan with Wesson oil and place tortilla in pan.

Brush top of second tortilla with oil.

Place in oven and bake until both sides are golden, about 6 minutes.

Cut tortilla into 6 pieces and place on serving platter. Garnish with Yellow Tomato Salsa.

For Lobster White Cheddar Mix Combine all ingredients in mixing bowl.

Refrigerate until ready to use.

For Quesadilla Cheese Mix Mix all ingredients.

Refrigerate until ready to use.

Suggested Wine: Santa Barbara Winery Chardonnay 2002 Reserve

Lobster-Brie Quesadilla

1½ cups **Lobster-Quesadilla Mix**
  (see recipe below)

12 **10" Chili-Cilantro Flour Tortillas**

⅔ cup **Caramelized Sweet Onion**
  (see recipe below)

12 oz. **brie cheese**, sliced thin

½ cup **Wesson Oil**, for cooking

1 cup **Roasted Corn Poblano Relish**
  (see page 183)

Lobster Brie Mix

2 cloves **garlic**, roasted and
  very finely chopped

1 **Poblano pepper**, roasted,
  peeled and finely chopped

1 **red pepper**, roasted, peeled and
  finely chopped

2 teaspoons **cilantro**, finely chopped

¼ teaspoon **kosher salt**

1 lb. **lobster meat**, chopped into
  ½" pieces

Caramelized Sweet Onion

1 small **red sweet onion**, sliced thinly

2 tablespoons **olive oil**

2 tablespoons **butter**, melted

For Lobster Brie Mix Mix all ingredients.

For Caramelized Sweet Onion Combine oil and butter in large stainless steel saucepan and heat.

Add onions and cook until golden, about 5–6 minutes.

Preparation of Quesadilla for one serving

Preheat oven to 450°.

Place 2 tablespoons Caramelized Sweet Onion on tortilla.

Place ¼ cup Lobster Quesadilla Mix on top of onions.

Place 2 slices of brie on top of Lobster Quesadilla Mix. Top with second tortilla shell.

Brush oil in sauté pan and place tortilla in pan. Brush top layer of tortilla with oil.

Place tortilla in oven and cook until golden, about 6 minutes.

Cut in 6 pieces and place on serving platter. Garnish with Roasted Corn Poblano Relish over top of quesadilla.

Suggested Wine: Firestone Sauvignon Blanc 2003 Santa Barbara

Grilled Herb Flatbread *with* Basil Pesto *and* Four Cheeses

2	6" x 12" piece **Herb Flatbread Dough** (see page 48)
4	tablespoons **Basil Pesto** (see recipe below)
2	tablespoons **Sun-Dried Tomato Relish** (see page 182)
½	cup fresh **mozzarella cheese**, cut in julienne strips
½	cup **Quattro Formaggio Mix** (see recipe below)
2	tablespoons **Tomato Concasse** (see page 15)
2	teaspoons fresh **chives**, chopped

Quattro Formaggio Mix

(Makes 1 cup)

¼	cup **Parmesan cheese**, shredded
¼	cup **asiago cheese**, shredded
¼	cup aged **provolone cheese**, shredded
¼	cup **Romano cheese**, shredded

Basil Pesto *(Makes 1 cup)*

2	cloves **garlic**
½	teaspoon **salt**
½	cup **basil** leaves
2	tablespoons **pine nuts**
½	cup **olive oil**
¼	cup **Parmesan cheese**, freshly grated
1	teaspoon **Romano cheese**, freshly grated
2	tablespoons **butter**, softened

Preheat oven to 450°.

Place each Herb Flatbread Dough on grill and cook lightly on both sides at medium high heat.

Cool before processing.

Brush each dough with Basil Pesto.

Sprinkle 2 tablespoons Quattro Formaggio Mix on each cooled dough.

Evenly distribute ¼ cup fresh mozzarella strips on top of Quattro Formaggio Mix.

Sprinkle 2 tablespoons Quattro Formaggio Mix over top of mozzarella.

Sprinkle Sun-Dried Tomato Relish over top of cheese.

Top with Tomato Concasse.

Place in oven and bake until golden, about 6–8 minutes.

Cut each flatbread into 6 pieces widthwise and place on serving platter.

Top with chopped chives.

For Quattro Formaggio Mix Mix well.

For Basil Pesto Place garlic, salt, basil, pine nuts, and olive oil in the bowl of a food processor, fitted with the metal blade, and process until mixture is smooth.

Add cheeses and butter and process again until well combined.

Suggested Wine: Stags Leap Hawk Crest Cabernet Sauvignon 2002 Napa Valley

Arugula-Walnut Pesto Flatbread

2   6" x 12" piece **Herb Flatbread Dough** (see page 48)

½   cup **Arugula Walnut Tomato Pesto Sauce** (see recipe below)

½   cup **provolone cheese**, shredded

1   **red pepper**, roasted and peeled, finely julienned

1   **yellow pepper**, roasted and peeled, finely julienned

1   medium **plum tomato**, seeded, cut into 1" small dice

Arugula-Walnut Tomato Pesto
(Makes 1 cup)

½   cup **arugula**, cleaned and stemmed

2   teaspoons **sun dried tomatoes**, chopped

2   tablespoons **olive oil**

1   tablespoon **walnuts**

¼   teaspoon fresh **thyme**

1   clove **garlic**, roasted and finely chopped

2   teaspoons **Parmesan cheese**, grated

¼   teaspoon **kosher salt**

⅛   teaspoon **white pepper**

1   tablespoons **butter**, softened

Preheat oven to 450°.

Grill each Herb Flatbread on both sides at medium high heat and let rest until cool.

Brush ¼ cup Arugula Walnut Tomato Pesto Sauce over each flatbread.

Sprinkle 2 tablespoons of the provolone cheese over sauce.

Place roasted peppers on top of cheese.

Sprinkle with remaining 2 tablespoons of the provolone cheese over roasted peppers on each flatbread.

Top with plum tomatoes.

Place in oven and cook until cheese is golden and bubbly, about 10 minutes.

Cut into 6 slices and place on serving platter.

For Arugula-Walnut Tomato Pesto In blender, combine arugula, tomatoes, olive oil, walnuts, thyme, salt, pepper, butter and garlic and blend until smooth.

Add Parmesan cheese and blend.

Refrigerate until ready to use.

Suggested Wine: Beringer Pinot Noir 2001 Napa Valley

Littleneck Clam and Sausage Flatbread

2	6" x 12" piece **Herb Flatbread** (see page 48)
½	cup **Basil Pesto** (see page 45)
½	cup **asiago cheese**, shredded
½	cup **white cheddar cheese**, shredded
12	pieces **littleneck clams**, steamed, out of shell
½	cup **Italian Fennel Sausage**, cooked, crumbled
1	**red pepper**, roasted, finely julienned
1	**yellow pepper**, roasted, finely julienned
⅛	teaspoon **red pepper flakes**

Preheat oven to 450°.

Grill each Herb Flatbread on both sides on medium high heat. Let rest until cool.

Brush with ¼ cup pesto sauce on each flatbread.

Add 2 tablespoons of each cheese on top of Basil Pesto on each flatbread.

Spread 6 clams and ¼ cup sausage evenly over pesto on each flatbread.

Add red and yellow peppers evenly on each flatbread.

Add 2 tablespoons of the cheese on top of peppers.

Sprinkle with red pepper flakes.

Place in oven and cook until golden and cheese is bubbling, about 10 minutes.

Cut in 6 slices and place on serving platter.

For Basil Pesto Place garlic, salt, basil, pine nuts, and olive oil in the bowl of a food processor, fitted with the metal blade, and process until mixture is smooth.

Add cheeses and butter and process again until well combined.

Suggested Wine: Saintsbury "Garnet" Pinot Noir 2001 Carneros

Herb Flatbread Dough

1	cup warm **water**
1	package ¼ oz. **dry yeast**
2	teaspoons **sugar**
1½	teaspoons **kosher salt**
2	tablespoons **olive oil**
3	cups **high gluten flour**
3	teaspoons fresh **basil**, chopped
3	teaspoons fresh **thyme**, chopped
3	teaspoons fresh **chives**, chopped
3	teaspoons fresh **rosemary**, chopped

Mix warm water, sugar, salt and olive oil to dissolve yeast in mixer bowl.

Add herbs and flour and mix about 5 minutes with dough hook, or until dough is of a smooth consistency.

Remove from mixer, cut and portion into 4 balls for each flatbread. Brush with oil to retain moisture.

Shape each one in long shaped piece.

Place them on a cookie sheet and let rest for one hour.

Roll each dough ball into rectangle shape 6" x 12" and refrigerate until ready to use.

Salads

The markets today are so full of tempting greens and a variety of vegetables that making a salad has come a long way from a chunk of lettuce with a spoonful of dressing. I've given a sampling of different salads in this chapter that would be fun and challenging, and would add some great ideas for your summer parties. They can complement your dinner, be your dinner or even your dessert. Experiment with the dressings and come up with your own combinations that will add to your culinary adventures!

Tuscan Pear Salad

8   cups **Bibb lettuce**, torn in large pieces

½   cup **Gorgonzola cheese**, crumbled

¼   cup **Sugar Walnuts**
     (see recipe below)

16   slices **Caramelized Pears**
     (see recipe below)

½   cup **Herb-Balsamic Vinaigrette**
     (see page 64)

Caramelized Pears

2   **pears**, peeled and cored,
     cut into 8 pieces each

½   cup **honey**

Sugar Walnuts

½   cup **walnut** pieces

2   tablespoons **butter**, melted

1   tablespoon **sugar**

Clean and tear Bibb lettuce. Place on serving plate.

Sprinkle Gorgonzola cheese and Sugar Walnuts over top of greens.

Top each salad with 4 pear slices.

Drizzle with Herb-Balsamic Vinaigrette.

For Caramelized Pears   Place pears and honey in large sauté pan.

Cook over high heat until pears turn a golden color and liquid has evaporated.

For Sugar Walnuts   Preheat oven to 350°.

Toss walnut pieces with butter and sugar. Place on cookie sheet.

Bake in oven for 10 minutes.

Cool and place in plastic airtight container.

Shrimp *and* Scallop Creole Spinach Salad

16	large **shrimp**, tail off, peeled and deveined
16	medium **scallops**
4	teaspoons **butter**, melted
1	tablespoon **Paul Prudhomme Cajun Seasoning**, for dusting
8	cups **spinach**, stemmed and washed
4	teaspoons **sesame seeds**, toasted
1	**red pepper**, julienned ¼"
1	**yellow pepper**, julienned ¼"
4	strips **bacon**, crisply cooked, chopped into ½" pieces
1	cup **Creole Mustard Bacon Vinaigrette** (see recipe below)
½	cup **mushrooms**, thinly sliced
8	**red grape tomatoes**
8	**yellow teardrop tomatoes**

Creole Mustard Bacon Vinaigrette
(Makes 2 cups)

2	tablespoons **Creole mustard**
⅓	cup **cider vinegar**
1	tablespoon fresh **chives**, finely chopped
1	teaspoon **salt**
½	teaspoon **black pepper**
1½	cups **olive oil**
1	lb. **bacon**, chopped into ½" pieces
¼	teaspoon **Paul Prudhomme Cajun Seasoning**
1	**garlic** clove, finely chopped
1	tablespoon fresh **lemon juice**

Lightly brush shrimp and scallops with butter and dust with Paul Prudhomme Cajun Seasoning.

Place in skillet on high heat and sear them until they are cooked and golden.

Place remaining ingredients in mixing bowl with dressing and mix well.

Place on serving plate.

Top with cooked shrimp and scallops. Sprinkle with sesame seeds.

For Creole Mustard Bacon Vinaigrette Place bacon in sauté pan and render completely until crispy.

Remove bacon from pan with slotted spoon and put into mixing bowl.

Add ¼ cup bacon grease to bowl.

Add all other ingredients to bowl and mix well. Warm dressing when ready to serve.

Suggested Wine: Jekel Gravelstone Chardonnay 2002 Monterey

Greek-Style Romaine Salad

8   cups **romaine salad greens**, cleaned, cut in large chunks

2   cups **English seedless cucumber**, cut in half, sliced on bias

1   small **red onion**, finely julienned

16   **red grape tomatoes**, cut in half

1   cup **feta cheese**, crumbled

½   cup assorted **Greek olives****

1   cup **Creamy Dijon-Oregano Vinaigrette** (see recipe below)

12   pieces **Feta Cheese Croutons**, warm (see recipe below)

8   **artichoke hearts**, quartered

Feta Cheese Croutons *(Makes 8 pieces)*

3   sheets **Fillo dough**

8   tablespoons **feta cheese**, crumbled

     butter, melted for brushing Fillo

Creamy Dijon Oregano Vinaigrette
(Makes 1½ cups)

1   **egg yolk**

2   tablespoons **red wine vinegar**

2   teaspoons **Dijon mustard**

1   small **garlic** clove, finely chopped with **kosher salt**

1   tablespoon fresh **lemon juice**

1   cup **extra virgin olive oil**

½   teaspoon **kosher salt**

¼   teaspoon **black pepper**

2   teaspoons fresh **oregano**, finely chopped

Warm Feta Cheese Croutons in oven at 350° until crispy.

Place romaine, cucumbers, red onion, tomatoes, olives and artichoke hearts in mixing bowl and toss with 1 cup of dressing.

Place on serving plate, making sure some of the ingredients remain on top of salad.

Place Feta Cheese Croutons on top of salad in pinwheel fashion.

Top with crumbled feta cheese and drizzle extra dressing over top.

For Feta Cheese Croutons Lay out one sheet of Fillo dough on work surface and brush with melted butter. Repeat with the other sheets.

Cut into 8 square pieces.

Place 1 tablespoon feta cheese onto each square and fold into triangle. Brush outside with melted butter.

Place in refrigerator until ready to use.

For Creamy Dijon Oregano Vinaigrette In food processor combine egg yolks, vinegar, lemon juice, mustard and garlic. Mix well.

Slowly add olive oil in steady stream while stirring or with processor running.

Add oregano, salt and pepper. Mix well.

*You can find these and other types of olives in the deli section of most markets.

Suggested Wine: Baileyana Winery Sauvignon Blanc, Paragon Vineyard 2001

Return to the Common Grill

Shanghai Chicken Salad

1½ lbs. **chicken breast**, poached in
    chicken stock
1   cup **Chicken Stock**
    (see page 16)
¼   lb. **angel hair pasta**
4   teaspoons **curry powder**, for pasta
1   cup **Mesclun (spring mix) greens**
¼   cup **spinach leaves**
¼   cup **napa cabbage**, chopped into
    1" pieces
½   cup **English cucumber**, peeled,
    finely julienned
4   tablespoons **green onion**, cut on bias
1   tablespoon **cilantro**, chopped
¼   cup **carrot**, finely julienned
¼   cup **red bell pepper**, finely julienned
½   cup **pea pods**, finely julienned
4   teaspoons **honey roasted nuts**,
    chopped
4   teaspoons **sesame seeds**, toasted
1   cup **Chinese Mustard Vinaigrette**
    (see recipe below)

Chinese Mustard Vinaigrette
(Makes 2 cups)
2   **garlic** cloves
2   tablespoons **peanut butter**, smooth
¼   teaspoon **sugar**
¼   teaspoon **Chinese mustard**
½   cup **soy sauce**
½   cup **rice wine vinegar**
4   tablespoons **hot pepper oil**
½   cup **sesame oil**

Poach chicken breasts in chicken stock, cool and trim any fat. Julienne chicken breasts into ½" strips.

Cook angel hair pasta and cool in cold water, drain and toss with curry powder.

Refrigerate until ready to use.

Toss greens, spinach and napa cabbage with ½ cup of Chinese Mustard Vinaigrette and place on each individual serving plate.

Place curry noodles, poached chicken and vegetables in mixing bowl and toss with remaining vinaigrette, place on top of greens.

Top with honey roasted nuts and toasted sesame seeds.

For Chinese Mustard Vinaigrette Place all ingredients except oils into blender or food processor and combine well.

Slowly add oils and emulsify well.

Refrigerate until ready to use.

Suggested Wine: Handley Cellars Gewürztraminer 2002 Anderson Valley, Mendocino

Fresh Summer Fruit Salad *with*
Strawberry Honey Mint Dressing

1	**pineapple**, fresh
1	**papaya**, peeled, cut into 12 slices, ½" thick
16	**blackberries**
24	**raspberries**
1	**mango**, peeled, cut into 12 slices ½" thick
12	**strawberries**
1½	cups **honeydew melon**, large cube
1½	cups **cantaloupe**, large cube
4	cups **Bibb lettuce**, torn
1½	cups **Strawberry Honey Mint Dressing** (see recipe below)
4	sprigs fresh **mint**

Strawberry Honey Mint Dressing

1	cup **Crème Fraîche**
1	cup **strawberries**, finely chopped
2	tablespoons **honey**
1	tablespoon fresh **mint**, finely chopped

Quarter pineapple lengthwise. Trim leaves and slice along rind and remove fruit.

Slice across fruit into ½" pieces and place back onto rind.

Line each serving plate with Bibb lettuce. Place one quarter of pineapple onto center of each serving plate.

Toss the rest of the fruit together and place next to the quartered pineapple on the platter.

Drizzle with Strawberry Honey Mint Dressing and garnish with mint sprig.

For Strawberry Honey Mint Dressing Whip all ingredients together well, using a wire whip.

Keep dressing chilled at all times.

Suggested Wine: Beringer Alluvium Blanc 2001 Knight's Valley

Warm Spinach Salad

4	4 oz. pieces **grilled chicken breast**, thinly sliced
4	pieces **Goat Cheese Fritter**, warm (see recipe below)
8	cups **baby spinach**, cleaned and stemmed
1	small **red onion**, finely julienned
1	cup **Bacon-Balsamic Vinaigrette**, warm (see opposite page)
24	slices **Caramelized Pears** (see page 50)
1	cup **Sugar Pecans** (see recipe below)

Goat Cheese Fritter

1	tablespoon **olive oil**
1	teaspoon **garlic**, finely chopped
4	tablespoons **leeks**, finely chopped
1	cup **goat cheese**, room temperature
2	tablespoons **Crème Fraîche**
½	cup **all-purpose flour**, for dusting
1½	cups **bread crumbs**
	olive oil for cooking fritter
	Egg Wash (see recipe below)

Egg Wash

1	**egg**
2	**tablespoons milk**

Sugar Pecans

½	cup **pecan halves**
2	tablespoons **sugar**
2	tablespoons **butter**, melted

Warm Goat Cheese Fritter in oven at 350°.

Toss spinach and red onions in mixing bowl with warm Bacon Balsamic Vinaigrette.

Place on serving platter.

Top with warm Goat Cheese Fritter in center of spinach.

Place grilled chicken breast around fritter.

Top with Caramelized Pears and Sugar Pecans.

For Goat Cheese Fritter Heat 1 tablespoon olive oil in sauté pan and add garlic and leeks and cook until soft.

Mix goat cheese, Crème Fraîche, garlic and leeks in mixing bowl and blend well.

Form goat cheese mixture into patties using ¼ cup of the mixture for each fritter.

Dust in flour.

Dip in egg wash and coat well in bread crumbs.

Lightly cook the fritters in olive oil until golden in color and set aside.

For Egg Wash Combine egg and milk and set aside.

For Sugar Pecans Preheat oven to 350°.

Toss pecans with butter and sugar.

Bake in oven for 10 minutes on cookie sheet.

Remove from oven and allow to cool.

Bacon-Balsamic Vinaigrette *(Makes 2 cups)*

1	cup **bacon,** chopped into ½" pieces
1	cup **olive oil**
⅔	cup **balsamic vinegar**
⅓	cup **shallots,** very finely chopped
2	tablespoons **garlic,** very finely chopped
3	tablespoons **brown sugar**

For Bacon-Balsamic Vinaigrette Cook bacon until well rendered. Remove bacon and reserve.

Add ¼ cup of bacon oil to sauté pan, add olive oil and heat.

Add shallots, garlic and brown sugar and cook until soft.

Add balsamic vinegar and mix well.

Add cooked bacon and mix well. Remove and refrigerate until ready to use.

Suggested Wine: Wild Horse Viognier 2002

Shrimp Scampi Tuscan Salad

4 cups **Mesclun (spring mix) greens**
½ cup **Lemon-Basil Vinaigrette**
    (see recipe below)
2 cups **White Bean Fennel Salad**
    (see opposite page)
16 pieces very large **shrimp**, peeled,
    deveined, tail off
½ cup **Parmesan**, shaved
4 teaspoons **chives**, chopped
12 pieces **Sun-Dried Tomato Foccacia**,
    1" x 4" (see page 86)
½ cup **Roasted Garlic Butter**
    (see page 14)

Roasted Lemon-Basil Vinaigrette
(Makes 2 cups)

Roasted Lemon Juice
4 whole **lemons**
¼ cup **kosher salt**
1 tablespoon **sugar**

Vinaigrette
¼ cup **Roasted Lemon Juice**
    (see recipe above)
2 tablespoons **champagne vinegar**
2 teaspoons **Dijon mustard**
1 cup **olive oil**
½ teaspoon **kosher salt**
¼ teaspoon **black pepper**
1 teaspoon fresh **chives**, finely chopped
1 tablespoon fresh **basil**, finely chopped

Toss greens with Lemon Basil Vinaigrette and place on individual serving plates.

Top with ½ cup White Bean Fennel Salad, placing 4 shrimp on top of each salad.

Top with shaved Parmesan and chopped chives.

Garnish with 3 pieces of warm Sun-Dried Foccacia bread around each salad.

Preparation of Shrimp Heat Roasted Garlic Butter in sauté pan.

Add shrimp and cook until done in center. Allow to cool.

For Roasted Lemon Juice Toss lemons with salt and sugar, place in baking dish and cover.

Place in oven at 350° for 45 minutes.

Let cool, cut lemons in half and juice them well.

For Vinaigrette Combine Roasted Lemon Juice, vinegar and mustard in food processor.

Add salt and pepper.

In slow steady stream add olive oil with food processor running. Mix in fresh herbs.

For White Bean Fennel Salad Combine all ingredients in mixing bowl.

Suggested Wine: Girard Sauvignon Blanc 2002 Napa Valley

White Bean Fennel Salad

(Makes 2 cups)

1	cup	**Navy beans**, cooked
¼	cup	**Tomato Concasse** (see page 15)
¼	cup	**fennel bulbs**, finely diced
2	tablespoons	**extra virgin olive oil**
2	teaspoons	fresh **lemon juice**
2	teaspoons	**sherry vinegar**
2	teaspoons	**balsamic vinegar**
½	teaspoon	**Dijon mustard**
1	tablespoon	fresh **chives**, chopped
1	tablespoon	**cilantro**, chopped
2	tablespoons	**green onions**, chopped
2	tablespoons	fresh **parsley**, chopped
½	teaspoon	**kosher salt**
⅛	teaspoon	**white pepper**

Blackened Steak Salad

4	6 oz. pieces **flat iron sirloin steak**
4	teaspoons **Paul Prudhomme Cajun Seasoning**, for dusting
8	cups **Mesclun (spring mix) greens**
1	small **red onion**, thinly sliced
1	cup **Jalapeño Cornbread Croutons** (see recipe below)
1	cup **Buttermilk Bacon Ranch** (see recipe below)
24	**red grape tomatoes**

Buttermilk Bacon Ranch
(Makes 1 cup)

1	cup **Buttermilk Ranch Dressing**
1	tablespoon **green onion**, finely chopped
3	strips **bacon**, chopped into ½" pieces

Jalapeño Cornbread Croutons
(Makes croutons for 6 salads)

1½	cups **Jiffy Mix Cornbread Mix**
1	cup **sharp cheddar cheese**, grated
1	whole **jalapeño pepper**, seeded, finely chopped
1½	cups **creamed corn**
5	**eggs**, beaten
½	teaspoon **salt**
1	cup **buttermilk**

Dust steaks with Cajun spices and blacken them in hot skillet to proper doneness. Slice thinly after cooking.

Place 2 cups mixed greens on individual serving plates and top with sliced sirloin.

Top with sliced onions, ¼ cup Jalapeño Cornbread Croutons and 6 red grape tomatoes for each salad.

Drizzle ¼ cup dressing over each salad.

For Buttermilk Bacon Ranch Render bacon completely and allow to cool.

Mix all ingredients in mixing bowl and refrigerate until ready to use.

For Jalapeño Cornbread Croutons Preheat oven to 300°.

Reserve ¼ cup cheddar cheese.

Place ¾ cups cheddar cheese and remaining ingredients into mixing bowl. Mix very well.

Spray bottom and sides of 8 x 10-inch pyrex baking dish with vegetable spray.

Pour batter into pan and spread evenly.

Sprinkle ¼ cup of reserved cheese over top of batter.

Place in oven and cook for 45 minutes until cooked through.

Allow to cool and cut into 1" cubes.

Place in oven for about 10–15 minutes until golden and crunchy.

Suggested Wine: Morro Bay Vineyards Merlot 2001

Shrimp Salad Sante Fe *with* Salsa Dressing

SERVES 4

¼	cup **water**	
¼	cup **Tequila**	
¼	cup fresh **lime juice**	
24	large **gulf shrimp**, peeled and deveined, tail off	
8	cups **mixed greens**	
4	large slices **red beefsteak tomatoes**, grilled, chopped into ½" pieces	
4	large slices **yellow beefsteak tomatoes**, grilled, chopped into 1" pieces	
1	cup **red peppers**, roasted and cut into 1" squares	
1	cup **avocado**, chopped into ½" pieces	
½	cup **Cotija cheese** or **Monterey Jack**, shredded	
4	6" **corn tortillas** cut into ¼" julienne strips, deep fried	
1	cup Salsa Vinaigrette (see recipe below)	

Salsa Vinaigrette *(Makes 1 cup)*

⅔	cup **Tomato-Red Pepper Salsa** (see page 184)	
1	clove **garlic**	
2	tablespoons **red wine vinegar**	
2	tablespoons fresh **lemon juice**	
¼	teaspoon **cumin**	
1	sprig fresh **parsley**	
½	**jalapeño pepper**, halved, seeded, stem removed	
⅓	cup **olive oil**	

Mix water, Tequila and fresh lime juice in a saucepan. Bring to medium heat.

Add shrimp and poach until cooked through, about 5 minutes. Cool.

Place salad greens, tomatoes and red pepper in mixing bowl, add vinaigrette and mix well.

Place mixture onto serving plates.

Place avocado and cheese on top of greens.

Add 6 pieces of shrimp for each salad on top of cheese.

Garnish with tortilla strips.

For Salsa Vinaigrette Place Tomato Red Pepper Salsa, garlic cloves, red wine vinegar, lemon juice, cumin, parsley and jalapeño pepper in blender cup and emulsify.

Add olive oil in a steady stream until well mixed.

Refrigerate until ready to use.

Suggested Wine: Carneros Creek Pinot Noir 2002 Carneros

Roasted Tomato-Garlic Vinaigrette

8	**garlic** cloves, roasted
4	**plum tomatoes**, cut in half
2	tablespoons **olive oil**
4	tablespoons **red wine vinegar**
½	small **red onion**, chopped
2	tablespoons **honey**
2	tablespoons fresh **lime juice**
1	teaspoon **sea salt**
½	teaspoon **black pepper**

Preheat oven to 350°.

Place garlic cloves, plum tomatoes and 1 tablespoon olive oil in roasting pan and place in oven. Cook for 45 minutes until garlic is golden and tomatoes are cooked. Allow to cool.

Place all ingredients in food processor except olive oil and purée.

With the motor running, slowly add the remaining 1 tablespoon olive oil until emulsified.

Refrigerate until ready to use.

Makes 1 cup

Sweet Balsamic Vinaigrette

1	cup **olive oil**
⅓	cup **white balsamic vinegar**
1½	teaspoons **garlic**, chopped
1½	tablespoons **sugar**
1½	tablespoons **dry mustard**
½	teaspoon **kosher salt**
¼	teaspoon cracked **black pepper**

Combine all ingredients in a mixing bowl.

Makes 2 cups

Herb-Balsamic Vinaigrette

2	tablespoons **country Dijon mustard**
1	cup **olive oil**
¼	cup **balsamic vinegar**
2	tablespoons fresh **chives**, finely chopped
1	teaspoon fresh **thyme**, stems removed, finely chopped
1	teaspoon fresh **basil**, finely chopped
1	teaspoon **salt**
⅛	teaspoon **black pepper**

Combine all ingredients and mix well.

Refrigerate until ready to use.

Makes 2 cups

Mango-Black Pepper Vinaigrette

¼	cup **red wine vinegar**
1	teaspoon **garlic**, finely chopped
1	teaspoon crushed **black pepper**
2	tablespoons **cilantro**, chopped
½	teaspoon **sea salt**
⅓	cup **olive oil**
1	**mango**, peeled and pitted, ½ puréed, ½ diced into ¼" pieces

Add all ingredients to food processor, except olive oil and diced mango. Mix well.

With machine running, slowly add olive oil.

Turn off machine and mix in the diced mango. Refrigerate.

Makes 2 cups

Sun-Dried Tomato Vinaigrette

4	**sun-dried tomatoes**
2	**plum tomatoes**, seeded, chopped into ½" pieces
2	tablespoons **water**
¼	teaspoon **salt**
⅛	teaspoon cracked **black pepper**
4	tablespoons **cider vinegar**
2	tablespoons fresh **lemon juice**
1	tablespoon **Dijon mustard**
¼	teaspoon **salt**
1	cup **olive oil**

Place sun-dried tomatoes, chopped plum tomatoes, water, salt and cracked black pepper in saucepan and cook slowly for 15 minutes. Cool.

Transfer to food processor and purée. Place in mixing bowl.

Add remaining ingredients except oil and mix very well with a whisk.

Add olive oil gradually and then chill until ready to use.

Makes 2 cups

Brunch

There is nothing better on a weekend morning than making it special, bypassing the cereal and turning up the griddle. In this chapter I've included some wonderful recipes that are great for the family or qualify equally for company: delicious pancakes, waffles, French toast, omelets, quesadillas. But, I must tell you that the Crab Cake Melt is our #1 selling item on our Brunch menu.

Peppered Smoked Salmon *with* **Poached Egg**

8	**Smoked Salmon Cakes** (see recipe below)
8	**eggs**, poached
8	pieces **multi-grain toast**, buttered
4	tablespoons **Key Lime Aioli** (see recipe below)
4	teaspoons fresh **chives**, chopped
	fresh **fruit** garnish

Smoked Salmon Cakes

½	lb. peppered **smoked salmon**
½	lb. **Yukon gold potatoes**, peeled, cooked, grated
1	**egg**, lightly beaten
1	tablespoon **butter**, melted
½	teaspoon **kosher salt**
¼	teaspoon **black pepper**

Key Lime Aioli *(Makes 1 cup)*

1	**egg yolk**
4	teaspoons fresh **basil**, chopped
1½	teaspoons **garlic**, chopped
¼	cup **olive oil**
⅛	teaspoon **salt**
	pinch **white pepper**
2	tablespoons **key lime juice**

Broil Smoked Salmon Cakes until golden brown, place on serving platter.

Place poached eggs on top of each cake.

Drizzle Key Lime Aioli over top of eggs.

Garnish with multi grain toast, jam and fresh fruit.

Sprinkle with chopped chives.

For Smoked Salmon Cakes Combine all ingredients together and mix well.

Using a ¼ cup for each cake, form into patties and brush with melted butter.

Refrigerate until ready to use.

For Key Lime Aioli In a food processor combine egg yolks, basil, garlic and mix well. With machine running, slowly pour in olive oil and process until smooth.

Add salt, white pepper and key lime juice, mix well.

Reserve until ready to use.

Return to the Common Grill

Maryland Crab Cake Melt

8   halves **English muffin**, toasted
8   **eggs**, poached
8   **Maryland Crabcakes** (see recipe below)
8   teaspoons **butter**, melted
4   tablespoons **Key Lime Aioli**
       (see opposite page)
4   tablespoons **Tomato Concasse**
       (see page 15)
8   slices **yellow cheddar cheese**
1   teaspoon fresh **chives**, chopped
       fresh **fruit** garnish

Maryland Crab Cake Mix
(Makes 8 cakes)
1   lb. jumbo **lump crab meat**
¼   cup **bread crumbs**, dry
½   cup **mayonnaise**
1   **egg**
1   tablespoon fresh **chives**, chopped
1   teaspoon **Lea & Perrins**
1   teaspoon **mustard**
1   teaspoon **salt**
¼   teaspoon **white pepper**
1   teaspoon **red pepper**, finely chopped

Brush English muffin with Key Lime Aioli and toast under broiler.

Brush Maryland Crab Cakes with butter and cook until golden under broiler.

Placed sliced cheddar cheese onto muffin and melt under broiler.

Place crab cake onto muffin and place on serving plate and sprinkle with Tomato Concasse.

Top with poached egg and garnish with chopped chives and fresh fruit.

Drizzle with Key Lime Aioli.

For Maryland Crab Cake Mix Combine all ingredients together and mix well.

Using a ¼ cup measure, form into 8 crab cakes.

Banana-Pecan Buttermilk Pancakes

Banana Pancake Mix, ¼ cup
    per pancake (see recipe below)
Caramelized Bananas, sliced on
    bias ½" (see opposite page)
½   cup **pecans**, toasted
1   cup **Cinnamon Crème Fraîche**
    (see opposite page)
    powdered **sugar**, for dusting
    pure maple syrup, warm

Banana Buttermilk Pancake Mix
(Makes 16 medium pancakes)
2   cups **all-purpose flour**
4   teaspoons **baking powder**
1   teaspoon **baking soda**
4   tablespoons **brown sugar**
1   teaspoon **salt**
¼   teaspoon **cinnamon**
2   cups **bananas**, very ripe, mashed
2   teaspoons fresh **lemon juice**
2   **eggs**, separated
1   cup **Crème Fraîche**
1   cup **buttermilk**
2   teaspoons **vanilla extract**
⅓   cup **butter**, melted
2   teaspoons **lemon zest**

Ladle pancake batter onto hot griddle and cook at 375° on both sides until golden.

Place on serving platter in pinwheel arrangement.

Top with Caramelized Bananas and pecans.

Drizzle Cinnamon Crème Fraîche on top of pancakes and dust with powdered sugar.

Serve with warm maple syrup.

For Banana Buttermilk Pancake Mix Sprinkle bananas with lemon juice. Mix.

Sift all dry ingredients in a mixing bowl.

Combine bananas, egg yolks, Crème Fraîche, buttermilk, vanilla, melted butter and lemon zest in another bowl.

Add to dry ingredients and mix well.

Whip egg whites until soft peaks form.

Fold egg whites into batter mix. Do not over mix.

Refrigerate until ready to use.

For Caramelized Bananas Melt butter in sauté pan over high heat until foam subsides.

Place bananas, cut side down, in pan and cook about 1–2 minutes.

Remove from heat.

Add brown sugar and Myers Dark Rum

Return to heat and continue to sauté about 30 seconds.

Add water, cinnamon, nutmeg, salt and cook over medium high heat until sauce has thickened.

Caramelized Bananas
(Makes enough for 4 servings)

2   tablespoons **butter**
3   **bananas**, halved lengthwise,
      then crosswise
2   tablespoons **dark brown sugar**
¼   cup **Myers Dark Rum**
1   tablespoon **water**
½   teaspoon **nutmeg**
½   teaspoon **cinnamon**
      pinch **salt**

Cinnamon Crème Fraîche
(Makes 1 cup)

1   cup **Crème Fraîche**
½   teaspoon **ground cinnamon**
2   tablespoons **sugar**
1   teaspoon **vanilla extract**

Remove from pan and place on cookie sheet and allow to cool.

Sprinkle banana pieces with sugar and use blow torch to caramelize like you would a crème brulee.

For Cinnamon Crème Fraîche Place all ingredients in mixing bowl and whip until stiff.

Refrigerate until ready to serve.

Roasted Chicken-Andouille Sausage Hash Cakes

8   **Roasted Chicken Hash Cakes,**
        ¼ cup per cakes (see opposite page)
1   cup **Diablo Pepper Sauce**
        (see recipe below)
8   **eggs**, poached
4   tablespoons **Jalapeño Crème Fraîche**
        (see page 35)
4   teaspoons fresh **chives**, chopped
8   pieces **multi-grain toast**, grilled
        fresh **fruit** garnish

Diablo Pepper Sauce *(Makes 2 cups)*
1   tablespoon **olive oil**
¼   cup **red bell pepper**, chopped
        into ¼" pieces
¼   cup **yellow bell pepper** chopped
        into ¼" pieces
¼   cup **green bell pepper**, chopped
        into ¼" pieces
1   cup **Diablo Sauce**
        (see recipe below)

Diablo Sauce *(Makes 2 cups)*
3   tablespoons **olive oil**
½   piece **jalapeño pepper**, seeded,
        finely chopped
1   clove **garlic**, finely chopped
2   tablespoons **bread crumbs**
1   teaspoon **sherry wine**
1   cup **crushed tomatoes**
¼   cup **tomato sauce**
¼   cup **tomato juice**

Warm Roasted Chicken Hash Cakes under broiler until golden brown.

Ladle Diablo Pepper Sauce over top of hash cakes.

Place a poached egg on top of each sauce-covered hash cake.

Drizzle with Jalapeño Crème Fraîche and top with chopped chives.

Garnish with fresh fruit and 2 slices of toast.

Serve with jam.

For Diablo Pepper Sauce   Heat oil in saucepan.

Add peppers and cook until soft.

Add Diablo Sauce and mix well. Heat on low heat to warm and remove from stove.

Keep warm until ready to serve.

For Diablo Sauce   Place the olive oil into saucepan and heat.

Add the pepper/garlic mixture to the hot oil, remove from stove and mix well, return to stove and add the bread crumbs and mix well.

Add the sherry wine to the saucepan.

Add the crushed tomatoes and bring to a boil.

Add the tomato sauce and the tomato juice, mix well and cook for 5 minutes. Remove from stove and refrigerate.

Roasted Chicken Hash Cakes Mix
(Serves 4)

1	tablespoon **butter**, melted
2	tablespoon **red onion**, finely chopped
2	tablesspoons **red bell pepper**, finely chopped
2	tablespoons **yellow bell pepper**, finely chopped
1	clove **garlic**, roasted, finely chopped
¼	teaspoon **Paul Prudhomme Cajun Seasoning**
4	oz. **Andouille sausage**, finely chopped
4	oz. **roasted chicken**, finely chopped
2	cups **Potato Leek Cake Mix** (see page 149)
2	**eggs**

For Roasted Chicken Hash Cakes Mix Place butter in saucepan and heat.

Add red onion, peppers, roasted garlic, Paul Prudhomme Cajun Seasoning and cook until soft.

Add Andouille sausage and roasted chicken and mix well. Cook for 3–4 minutes.

Remove from stove and allow to cool.

When cool add mixture to Potato Leek Cake Mix.

Add eggs and mix well.

Using a ¼ cup portion, form into cakes and refrigerate until ready to serve.

Chorizo-Jack Quesadilla

1 cup **Monterey Jack cheese**, shredded
1 cup **Chorizo sausage**, cooked, crumbled
1 cup **Chipotle Salsa** (see recipe below)
¼ cup **olive oil**
4 tablespoons **jalapeño slices**, pickled
8 **eggs**
4 teaspoons fresh **chives**, chopped
4 tablespoons **Jalapeño Crème Fraîche** (see page 35)
8 6" flour **tortillas**

Chipotle Salsa *(Makes 1 cup)*
1 tablespoon **olive oil**
¼ cup **red onion**, thinly sliced
1 **garlic** clove, finely chopped
⅔ cup **crushed tomatoes**, diced
½ piece **jalapeño pepper**, chopped
½ piece **Chipotle pepper**, chopped
2 teaspoons **cilantro**, chopped
¼ cup **black beans**, cooked

Preparation for each serving Preheat oven to 450°.

Brush one side of one tortilla with ¼ cup Chipotle Salsa.

Top with ¼ cup Monterey Jack cheese and ¼ cup Chorizo sausage.

Place the other tortilla on top and press down.

Brush tortillas with vegetable oil and place in sauté pan.

Place in oven and bake until golden.

Lightly scramble eggs with jalapeño and chopped chives.

Place eggs in center of serving plate.

Cut tortilla in four pieces and place around eggs.

Drizzle with Jalapeño Crème Fraîche.

For Chipotle Salsa Heat oil. Add onions and garlic. Cook until softened.

Add tomatoes, jalapeño and Chipotle pepper. Bring to a boil. Reduce heat to low, simmer 10 minutes.

Purée 1 cup of salsa and add back to remaining salsa. Add cilantro.

Add black beans and mix well.

Pear Maple Waffles

1   cup **pears**, peeled, cut into
         small pieces
1½   cups **all-purpose flour**
½   teaspoon **baking soda**
½   tablespoon **baking powder**
½   teaspoon **salt**
½   teaspoon **cinnamon**
½   teaspoon **nutmeg**
3   **eggs**, separated
2   tablespoons **butter**, melted
¼   cup **maple syrup**
1¼   cups **buttermilk**
¼   cup **apple cider**
        Pear-Walnut Topping
         (see recipe below)
        powdered sugar, for dusting
        maple syrup, warm

Pear-Walnut Topping
4   tablespoons **butter**, softened
2   cups **pears**, thinly sliced
¼   cup **walnut** pieces
¼   cup **golden raisins**
¼   cup **brown sugar**
¼   cup hot **water**

Poach pears in water until tender.

Mix dry ingredients together well.

Whip egg yolks, maple syrup, butter, buttermilk and apple cider. Mix with cooked pears and add to dry ingredients and mix well.

Whip egg whites until soft peaks are formed. Fold into other ingredients and mix well.

Pour 1 cup of batter into waffle iron and cook until golden.

Top with ¼ cup of Pear-Walnut Topping, sprinkle with powdered sugar and serve with warm maple syrup.

For Pear-Walnut Topping   Heat butter in saucepan.

Add pears and cook on high heat until golden, about 3 minutes.

Add walnuts, golden raisins, brown sugar and hot water and cook until slightly thickened.

Shrimp *and* Lobster Omelet

2   tablespoons **butter**, melted
12   **eggs**, beaten
16   medium **shrimp**, poached,
           peeled, deveined
1   cup **lobster meat**, large chop
1   cup **Monterey Jack cheese**, shredded
½   cup **Béarnaise Sauce**
           (see recipe below)
4   cups fresh **fruit**

Béarnaise Sauce *(Makes ½ cup)*
½   teaspoon **cracked pepper**
2   tablespoons **tarragon vinegar**
2   **egg yolks**
½   cup **butter**, melted
¼   teaspoon fresh **lemon juice**
1   teaspoon **water**
        pinch **cayenne pepper**
¼   teaspoon **tarragon** leaves, chopped
        pinch **salt**

Preparation for each serving Heat 2 teaspoons butter in sauté pan.

Add 3 beaten eggs and spread around entire pan. Allow eggs to cook slightly before adding shrimp and lobster.

Add 4 shrimp and ¼ cup lobster and spread on top of eggs and warm.

Add ¼ cup cheese and allow to melt.

Fold over and place on serving plate.

Drizzle Béarnaise Sauce over top of each omelet.

Serve with fresh fruit.

For Béarnaise Sauce Combine cracked pepper with vinegar and cook until you have reduced volume by ½.

Immediately remove from stove and strain into blender.

Add eggs slowly and blend on low.

Add melted butter very slowly. Drawn butter should be at the same temperature as the mixture so as not to break.

Add fresh lemon juice, water and cayenne pepper.

Add tarragon leaves.

Add salt.

Remove and keep warm until serving.

Baked French Toast *with* Peach Compote

Streusel Topping

¼	cup **almonds** sliced, toasted
2	tablespoons **brown sugar**
⅓	cup **rolled oats**
¼	cup **all-purpose flour**
½	teaspoon **cinnamon**
2	tablespoons **butter**, softened

Milk Batter

1	cup **milk**
3	**eggs**, beaten
¼	teaspoon **cinnamon**
⅛	teaspoon **vanilla extract**
¼	cup **sugar**

Baked French Toast

4	pieces large **loaf egg bread**, 1" thick, sliced on bias
2	cups **Peach Compote**, ½ cup each serving (see recipe below)
8	tablespoons **Streusel Topping** (see recipe above)
	powdered sugar, for dusting
	maple syrup, warm

Peach Compote *(Makes 1½ cups)*

¼	cup **brown sugar**
½	cup **peach nectar**
½	teaspoon **cloves**, ground
½	teaspoon **ginger**, ground
1	teaspoon **cinnamon**, ground
1	lb. **peaches**, peeled and sliced

For Streusel Topping Mix all ingredients together well.

For Milk Batter Mix all ingredients together well.

For Baked French Toast Slice bread on bias.

Submerge bread in milk batter for 30 seconds.

Place on griddle at 375° and cook on both sides until golden.

Top with 2 tablespoons of Streusel Topping and place in oven until topping browns, about 6–8 minutes.

Place on serving plate and ladle warm Peach Compote over the top of the French toast.

Sprinkle with powdered sugar and serve with maple syrup.

For Peach Compote Place brown sugar, peach nectar, cloves, ginger and cinnamon into a saucepan. Heat to boiling.

Reduce heat and simmer uncovered for 10 minutes.

Add peaches. Cook until slightly thickened. Keep warm.

Sandwiches

Everything we prepare at the restaurant starts with the freshest ingredients whether it's vegetables, poultry, fish or cheese. We then wrap it in the freshest bread and sauce it with one of our house specialties. Suddenly, the pedestrian sandwich becomes culinary art. These are just a few of the sandwiches we have used at the restaurant over the years. The Jamaican Jerk Chicken takes a little time, but is well worth the energy.

Jamaican Jerk Chicken Sandwich

1   6 oz. piece **skinless chicken breast**, marinated

2   slices **Monterey Jack cheese**

2   tablespoons **Honeyed Jalapeño Sauce** (see recipe below)

2   pieces **sourdough bread**

1   **pineapple** slice, ⅛" thick

Jamaican Jerk Marinade
(Makes ¾ cup for six chicken breasts)

½   cup **red onion**, finely chopped

2   teaspoons fresh **thyme**, chopped

1   teaspoon **allspice**

½   teaspoon **cinnamon**

1   **garlic** clove, finely chopped

2   **jalapeño peppers**, seeded, finely chopped

½   teaspoon cracked **black pepper**

1   tablespoon fresh **lime juice**

3   teaspoons **olive oil**

4   tablespoons **Myers Dark Rum**

Honeyed Jalapeño Sauce
(Makes ¾ cup for six sandwiches)

2   **jalapeño peppers**, seeded

4   tablespoons **honey**

4   teaspoons **garlic**, finely chopped

4   teaspoons **cilantro**, finely chopped

½   teaspoon **allspice**

½   teaspoon **cumin**

4   teaspoons **olive oil**

4   teaspoons **balsamic vinegar**

4   tablespoons fresh **lemon juice**

4   teaspoons **Creole mustard**

For Jamaican Jerk Marinade Combine all ingredients in food processor and purée into smooth paste. Add more rum if needed to thin paste.

Marinate chicken breast for 4 hours.

For Honeyed Jalapeño Sauce Combine all ingredients in food processor and purée until smooth.

Place in saucepan and cook until slightly thickened on medium heat and allow to cool.

Preparation of Sandwich Place chicken breast on grill and cook on both sides until done. Brush with Honeyed Jalapeño Sauce over top of chicken while cooking. Place cheese on top of chicken and melt.

Place pineapple on top of chicken breast.

Place on sourdough bread and garnish with side of Honeyed Jalapeño Sauce.

Whitefish Po' Boy Sandwich

1   4 oz. piece **whitefish**, skin removed
1   oz. **buttermilk**, for soaking
1   oz. **Cajun Batter Mix**, for dusting
       (see recipe below)
1   oz. **lettuce**, shredded
1   oz. **plum tomatoes**, chopped into
       ½" pieces
2   tablespoons **Remoulade Sauce**
       (see recipe below)
1   **Kaiser roll**

Cajun Batter Mix
1   cup **all-purpose flour**
1   cup **Drake's Fry Crisp Batter Mix**
1   tablespoon **Paul Prudhomme**
       Cajun Seasonings

Remoulade Sauce *(Makes 1 cup)*
8   oz. **mayonnaise**
2   tablespoons **celery**, finely chopped
1   tablespoon **green onions**,
       finely chopped
2   teaspoons **fresh parsley**, finely chopped
2   tablespoons **horseradish**
1   tablespoon **Creole mustard**
1   tablespoon **ketchup**
1   tablespoon **Lea & Perrins**
2   teaspoons **capers**, finely chopped
2   teaspoons **sweet gherkins pickles**,
       finely chopped
2   teaspoons **yellow mustard**
2   teaspoons **Tabasco**
2   teaspoons **garlic**, finely chopped
1   teaspoon **paprika**
½   teaspoon **salt**
2   teaspoons fresh **lemon juice**

Soak whitefish in buttermilk for 1 hour.

Dust whitefish in Cajun Batter Mix and place in deep fryer and cook until golden.

Brush Kaiser roll with Remoulade Sauce.

Add 1 tablespoon Remoulade Sauce to lettuce and chopped tomatoes and mix well.

Place lettuce and tomato mix on bottom of Kaiser roll, place whitefish on top of lettuce, drizzle with Remoulade Sauce.

For Cajun Batter Mix Mix together well and keep in airtight container.

For Remoulade Sauce Place ½ cup of mayonnaise in blender with all of the remaining ingredients and blend well.

Pour into mixing bowl and add the remaining ½ cup of mayonnaise and mix well.

Refrigerate until ready to use.

1	6 oz. piece **tuna**, ¾" thick
2	tablespoons **Nicoise Marinade** (see recipe below)
2	tablespoons **Tomato Concasse** (see page 15)
1	tablespoon **Herb Balsamic Vinaigrette** (see page 64)
1	cup **arugula**
2	tablespoons **pancetta**, julienned, cooked crisply
2	tablespoons **Lemon Garlic Aioli** (see recipe below)
2	pieces **Ciabatta Bread**, sliced ½" thick, grilled, fresh **fruit** garnish

Nicoise Marinade

(For 6 pieces of tuna)

½	cup **extra virgin olive oil**
1	sprig fresh **rosemary**, chopped
1	sprig fresh **thyme**, chopped
1	sprig fresh **oregano**, chopped
1	tablespoon **fennel seed**, crushed
¼	teaspoon **kosher salt**
	pinch **black pepper**

Lemon Garlic Aioli

(Makes 1½ cups)

2	cloves **garlic**
½	teaspoon **kosher salt**
2	**egg yolks**
2	tablespoons fresh **lemon juice**
½	teaspoon cracked **black pepper**
⅛	teaspoon **cayenne pepper**
1	tablespoon **lemon zest**
1	cup **olive oil**

Marinate tuna with Nicoise Marinade for two hours.

Grill tuna to liking. (I suggest rare to medium rare.)

Toss arugula, Tomato Concasse and pancetta with Herb Balsamic Vinaigrette.

Place half on bottom of one side of grilled bread.

Top with grilled tuna and add remaining arugula over top of tuna.

Top with other piece of grilled bread.

Garnish with fresh fruit and Lemon Garlic Aioli.

For Nicoise Marinade Preparation Combine all ingredients in bowl. Mix thoroughly.

Refrigerate until ready to use.

For Lemon Garlic Aioli Place garlic and kosher salt in food processor and process using short bursts until finely chopped.

Add egg yolks, lemon juice, black pepper and cayenne pepper. Mix well.

With machine running slowly drizzle in olive oil. Add lemon zest and process until blended.

Refrigerate until ready to use.

Grilled Vegetable Sandwich

2   slices **eggplant**, ½" x 3" sticks
2   slices **yellow squash**, sliced ½" thick
2   slices **zucchini**, sliced ½" thick
2   **asparagus spears**
1   quarter **yellow pepper**
1   quarter **red pepper**
½   **Portabella Mushroom**, sliced
2   tablespoons **Red Onion Apple Relish**
          (see page 181)
2   slices **fresh mozzarella cheese**,
          sliced thin
2   tablespoons **Herb Marinade**
          (see page 22)
1   oz. **arugula**
2   tablespoons **Tomato Concasse**
          (see page 15)
1   tablespoon **Herb Balsamic**
          Vinaigrette (see page 64)
1   piece **Grilled Herb Flatbread**
          (see page 45)
1   oz. **Basil Aioli**
          (see page 190)
        fresh **fruit** garnish

Preheat oven to 400°.

Prepare vegetables according to recipe and place on cookie sheet. Brush with Herb Marinade and place in oven to cook until vegetables are half done. Remove and cool.

Stack vegetables starting with portabella mushroom, followed by eggplant, yellow squash, zucchini, red and yellow peppers, and asparagus.

Top with Apple Onion Relish and sliced fresh mozzarella cheese.

Place in oven and cook until cheese has melted. Place on top of Grilled Herb Bread.

Add arugula and Tomato Concasse that has been tossed with Herb Balsamic Vinaigrette.

Roll tightly, slice in half on bias and place on serving plate.

Garnish with Basil Aioli and fresh fruit.

New England Lobster Roll

½ cup **New England Lobster Roll Salad**
(see recipe below)

¼ cup **Romaine lettuce**, finely julienned

2 tablespoons **Tomato Concasse**
(see page 15)

1 piece **French Baguette**,
6" long, grilled

1 tablespoon **Roasted Garlic Butter**
(see page 14)

fresh **fruit** garnish

New England Lobster Roll Salad
(Makes 2 cups for four sanwiches)

1 lb. **lobster meat**, chopped into
½" pieces

¼ cup **celery**, peeled, finely diced

¼ cup **red bell pepper**, finely diced

⅓ cup **Tarragon Aioli**
(see recipe below)

1 tablespoon **green onion**, sliced thinly

2 tablespoons **fresh parsley**,
finely chopped

½ teaspoon **kosher salt**

Tarragon Aioli *(Makes 1 cup)*

2 **egg yolks**

1 teaspoon **Dijon mustard**

1¼ cups **olive oil**

1 tablespoon fresh **lemon juice**

¼ teaspoon **kosher salt**

pinch **white pepper**

1 tablespoon fresh **tarragon**

1 teaspoon fresh **chives**

Slice a thin slice off the top of the baguette and discard.

Brush cut side of remaining bun with Roasted Garlic Butter.

Slice bun in half lengthwise.

Grill bread on bottom side and Roasted Garlic Butter side.

Toss lettuce and Tomato Concasse together and place on bottom of bread.

Mound ¼ cup New England Lobster Roll Salad on top of lettuce.

Place top of grilled baguette on top of lobster salad.

Garnish with fresh fruit.

For New England Lobster Roll Salad Toss all ingredients together. Mix well.

Refrigerate until ready to use.

For Tarragon Aioli Mix eggs and Dijon mustard in food processor.

Add the oil a little at a time, with food processor running.

Add lemon juice, salt, pepper, tarragon and chives. Mix well.

Refrigerate until ready to use.

Grilled Three Cheese Sandwich

2   oz. **Chevre cheese**
2   slices **white cheddar cheese**
2   slices **fontina cheese**
3   slices **plum tomatoes**, sliced ¼"
2   slices **multi-grain bread**
1   tablespoon **butter**, melted
       fresh **fruit** garnish

Brush bread with melted butter and grill.

Place Chevre, cheddar, fontina and sliced tomatoes on one side of bread and place other slice on top.

Place in oven at 400° and cook until cheese has melted, about 5–6 minutes.

Cut on diagonal and place on serving plate.

Garnish with fresh fruit.

Serves 1

Rosemary Foccacia Bread

1   lb. **Foccacia Bread Dough** (see page 21)
2   tablespoons fresh **rosemary**, finely chopped
½   teaspoon **kosher salt**
½   oz. **extra virgin olive oil**

Preheat oven to 350°.

Roll dough out to fit 6 x 8-inch baking dish and place in pan.

Sprinkle with chopped rosemary and kosher salt.

Drizzle extra virgin olive oil over top of dough.

Allow to rise to ¾", about 30 minutes.

Place in oven and cook until golden in color, about 30 minutes.

Allow to cool and cut into 6 square pieces.

Makes 6 pieces

Sun-Dried Tomato Foccacia

1   lb. **Foccacia Bread Dough** (see page 21)
2   tablespoons **Sun-Dried Tomato Relish** (see page 181)
½   teaspoon **kosher salt**
½   oz. **extra virgin olive oil**

Preheat oven to 350°.

Roll dough out to fit 6 x 8-inch baking dish and place in pan.

Sprinkle with sun-dried tomato relish and kosher salt.

Drizzle extra virgin olive oil over top of dough.

Allow to rise to ¾", about 30 minutes.

Place in oven and cook until golden in color, about 30 minutes.

Allow to cool and cut into 6 square pieces.

Makes 6 pieces

In this chapter of Fish and Seafood I tried to include a wide variety of things that would spark your creative juices. We have a great Paella in this chapter, as well as grilled fish dishes that are fantastic any time of the year. Most important is to demand the freshest seafood from your market.

Fish & Seafood

Seafood Gumbo

2	tablespoons **olive oil**
½	cup **red onions**, chopped ½"
¼	cup **celery**, chopped ½"
¼	cup **red pepper**, chopped ½"
¼	cup **yellow pepper**, chopped ½"
¼	cup **green pepper**, chopped ½"
1	tablespoon **salt**
1	teaspoon **black pepper**
1	cup **crushed tomatoes**
2	tablespoons **garlic**, finely chopped
1	tablespoon **green onions**, finely chopped
64	oz. **clam juice**
8	oz. **fish**, cut into 1" cubes (such as **salmon**, **halibut** or **grouper**)
1	teaspoon **Lea & Perrins**
½	teaspoon **Tabasco**
2	tablespoons fresh **basil**, finely chopped
1	teaspoon fresh **oregano**, finely chopped
1	teaspoon fresh **thyme**, finely chopped
1	cup **okra**, sliced
2	teaspoons Paul Prudhomme **Cajun Seasoning**
8	oz. **shrimp**, medium size, tail off
8	oz. **blue crabmeat**, jumbo
8	oz. **lobster meat**, chopped
1	teaspoon **File Gumbo Spice**
3	cups **Rice Pilaf** (see page 146)
6	teaspoons **green onions**, chopped

Heat oil in large saucepot.

Add red onions, celery and peppers and sauté for 3–5 minutes until soft.

Add salt, black pepper, tomatoes, garlic and green onions and sauté for five minutes.

Stir in clam juice.

Add fish, Lea & Perrins, Tabasco, basil, thyme and oregano.

Bring to a boil and cook for 10 minutes over high heat.

Reduce to medium heat and add okra and Paul Prudhomme Cajun Seasoning. Simmer for 15 minutes.

Skim the top of gumbo and turn heat to high and cook for 3 minutes.

Fold in shrimp, crabmeat and lobster. Reduce heat to medium and cook for 3 minutes.

Add File Gumbo Spice and simmer for 2–3 minutes. Remove from heat.

Place ½ cup rice in each serving bowl and ladle 1 cup gumbo around rice.

Top with chopped green onions.

Suggested Wine: Rochioli Pinot Noir 2002 Russian River Valley

Poached Salmon *with* Morels *and* Sautéed Arugula

4	6 oz. pieces **salmon fillets**, skinned
1	cup **white wine**
1	cup **water**
½	cup **olive oil**
8	cloves **garlic**, chopped very fine
1	cup **morel mushrooms**, cleaned, cut in half
4	cups **arugula**, cleaned, thick stems removed
1	cup **red teardrop tomatoes**, chopped 1"
1	cup **yellow teardrop tomatoes**
1	cup **Roasted Tomato Sauce** (see recipe below)

Roasted Tomato Sauce
(Makes 4 cups)

1	lb. **plum tomatoes**, halved
2	tablespoons **shallots**, chopped
3	cloves **garlic**
½	cup **olive oil**
¼	teaspoon **black pepper**
1	sprig fresh **thyme**
1	sprig fresh **chives**
1	sprig fresh **oregano**
2	tablespoons **balsamic vinegar**
½	teaspoon **salt**

Poach salmon in white wine and water for 8 minutes or until salmon has cooked.

In a separate pan heat oil until hot.

Add garlic and sauté briefly.

Add mushrooms and sauté until tender.

Add arugula and tomatoes and sauté until just wilted.

Place mushrooms, arugula and tomato mixture on serving plate.

Placed poached salmon on top of greens and ladle Roasted Tomato Sauce on top.

For Roasted Tomato Sauce Preheat oven to 450°.

Place tomatoes in heavy baking pan with shallots and garlic. Drizzle with olive oil. Sprinkle with black pepper and herbs.

Bake in oven for 30 minutes or until tomatoes are well done.

Remove from oven and place ingredients in food processor. Purée until well blended. Add vinegar and salt and purée again.

Refrigerate until ready to use.

Suggested Wine: Kenwood Pinot Noir 2000 Reserve Olivet

Grilled Ahi Tuna *with* Olive Mustard Butter *and* Three Bean Compote

4	8 oz. pieces **ahi tuna**, 1" thick
4	tablespoons **olive oil**
2	teaspoons **sea salt**
2	cups **Three Bean Compote** (see recipe below)
½	cup **Olive Mustard Butter** (see recipe below)
4	teaspoons fresh **chives**, finely chopped

Olive Mustard Butter *(Makes 1 cup)*

1	lb. **butter**, room temperature
¼	cup **black cured olives**, pitted
1	tablespoon **shallots**, roasted and chopped
1	tablespoon fresh **parsley**, chopped
1½	tablespoons **Dijon mustard**
1	teaspoon **sea salt**
¼	teaspoon **white pepper**

Three Bean Compote *(Makes 3 cups)*

⅔	cup **olive oil**
4	**garlic** cloves, finely chopped
¼	cup **red onion**, finely chopped
½	cup **plum tomatoes**, chopped ¼" dice
2	tablespoons fresh **chives**, chopped
1	tablespoon fresh **basil**, chopped
1	tablespoon fresh **rosemary**, chopped
4	tablespoons **balsamic vinegar**
⅓	cup **navy beans**, cooked
⅓	cup **kidney beans**, cooked
⅓	cup **black beans**, cooked
1	teaspoon **salt**
½	teaspoon **white pepper**

Brush tuna with olive oil and sprinkle with sea salt.

Place on grill at high heat and cook rare to medium rare, about 2–3 minutes on each side.

Place warm Three Bean Compote in center of each serving plate.

Place tuna on top of Three Bean Compote.

Spoon Olive Mustard Butter on top of fish.

Garnish with chopped chives.

For Olive Mustard Butter Place all ingredients in food processor and mix well.

Refrigerate until ready to use.

For Three Bean Compote Heat olive oil in large pot.

Add garlic and red onions and sauté until soft.

Add plum tomatoes, chives, basil and rosemary, mix well.

Stir in balsamic vinegar.

Add beans, salt and pepper. Cook for 15 minutes, remove from stove and keep warm until ready to serve.

Suggested Wine: J. Pinot Gris, 2001 Russian River Valley

Paella

1	cup **Paella Rice Pilaf** (see opposite page)
1	6 oz. piece **boneless chicken breast**
4	**littleneck clams**, cleaned
4	**mussels**, cleaned
2	oz. **Chorizo sausage** (2 pieces)
4	medium **shrimp**, peeled, deveined, tail on
2	1 oz. pieces **salmon**
2	1 oz. pieces **sea bass**
1	medium size **lobster tail**, split lengthwise
4	**asparagus spears**, trimmed
¼	cup **French beans**, trimmed
¼	cup fresh **peas**
1½	oz. **Lobster Stock** (see page 18)
1½	oz. **Chicken Stock** (see page 16)

Place Paella Rice Pilaf in center of paella pan.

In clockwise manner starting with the chicken breast place all ingredients around rice. Follow with sausage, mussels, clams, shrimp, salmon and sea bass.

Place lobster tail in center, meat facing down.

Top with asparagus, French beans and peas. Pour Lobster Stock and Chicken Stock over rice.

Cover and cook on open burner until clams are opened and everything is cooked, about 6–8 minutes.

Suggested Wine: MacMurray Ranch Pinot Noir 2000 Russian River Valley

Paella Rice Pilaf

½	cup **margarine**
⅓	cup **onion**
1	small **leek**, chopped
1	clove **garlic**, finely chopped
2	cups **Uncle Ben's Rice**, parboiled
1	teaspoon **kosher salt**
1½	cups **Lobster Stock** (see page 18)
1½	cups **Chicken Stock** (see page 16)
¼	teaspoon **saffron**
¼	cup **crushed tomatoes**

Preheat oven to 350°.

Melt margarine until hot.

Add onions, leeks and garlic and cook until translucent in color.

Add raw rice and salt and toss the rice for 2–3 minutes.

Pour both the Lobster and Chicken Stocks on the rice, mix well. Add saffron.

Bring rice to a boil.

Cover the pot with a piece of buttered wax paper that has been cut to size of pot. Cut hole in center to allow steam to escape.

Remove from stove and place in oven and cook for 17 minutes.

Add tomatoes to cooked rice and mix well.

Parmesan Crusted Whitefish *with* Lemon-Chive Butter
SERVES 4

4	6 oz. pieces **whitefish**, skinned
	milk, for soaking fish
2	cups **orzo pasta**, cooked
1	cup **lobster meat**, chopped
½	cup **crimini mushrooms**, sliced
½	cup **radicchio**, sliced
½	cup **Drake's Fry Crisp Batter Mix**
½	cup **tempura rice flour**
½	cup **Parmesan cheese**, grated
½	cup **Wesson Oil**, for sautéing
½	cup **Roasted Lemon-Chive Butter**
	(see recipe below)
½	cup **olive oil**
2	cups **Sautéed Spinach**
	(see page 145)
4	teaspoons fresh **chives**, chopped
4	**lemon wedges**

Roasted Lemon-Chive Butter
(Makes 1 cup)

½	lb. **butter**, softened
1	tablespoon fresh **chives**, finely chopped
¼	cup **butter**, melted
½	teaspoon **salt**
1	teaspoon **black pepper**
½	teaspoon **sugar**
2	tablespoons **Roasted Lemon Juice** (see page 58)

Soak whitefish fillets in milk for one hour.

Mix orzo pasta, lobster meat, mushrooms and radicchio together and refrigerate until ready to use.

Mix Drake's Fry Crisp Batter Mix, tempura rice flour and Parmesan cheese together.

Dust whitefish in Parmesan batter.

Place Wesson Oil in sauté pan and heat.

Cook whitefish until golden brown. Remove from pan.

Add Roasted Lemon-Chive Butter to pan and melt.

In a separate sauté pan place olive oil with orzo-lobster mix in oven to get warm.

Place orzo in center of serving plate.

Place whitefish on top of orzo.

Place Sautéed Spinach next to orzo and pour Roasted Lemon Chive Butter over top of whitefish.

Top with chopped chives and garnish with lemon wedge.

For Roasted Lemon Chive Butter Place butter in mixer bowl and whip until soft.

Add all other ingredients and mix well.

Refrigerate until ready to use.

Suggested Wine: St. Francis Chardonnay 2001 Sonoma

Grilled Salmon *with* Lobster Mashers

4	6 oz. pieces **salmon**, skinned
2	teaspoons **sea salt**
4	cups **Lobster Mashers**
	(see page 151)
½	lb. blanched **French beans**
1	cup **Roasted Yellow Tomato Leek Sauce** (see recipe below)
4	tablespoons **Basil-Garlic Oil** (see recipe below)
4	teaspoons fresh **chives** chopped
4	**lemon wedges**

Roasted Yellow Tomato Leek Sauce
(Makes 2 cups)

5	lbs. large **yellow tomatoes**, roasted, seeded, peeled and chopped
3	tablespoons **butter**
½	cup **extra virgin olive oil**
3	**garlic** cloves, finely chopped
⅓	cup **leeks**, chopped ¼"
3	tablespoons **tomato paste**
1	tablespoon fresh **basil**, finely chopped
2	tablespoons **sugar**
2	teaspoons **black pepper**

Brush salmon with olive oil and season with sea salt.

Place on grill and cook on one side 3–4 minutes.

Turn salmon and cook 3–4 minutes more or until done.

Place Lobster Mashers in center of serving plate.

Ladle Tomato Leek Sauce next to Lobster Mashers.

Place salmon on top of sauce leaning on Lobster Mashers.

Drizzle Basil-Garlic Oil over top of salmon.

Place warm French beans next to Lobster Mashers.

Top with chopped chives.

For Roasted Yellow Tomato Leek Sauce Preheat oven to 450°.

Cut tomatoes in half and remove the seeds.

Place cut side down and place in oven and roast until done, about 25 minutes.

Allow to cool.

Peel skins off tomatoes and chop in large chunks.

Place butter and olive oil in large saucepan and heat.

Sauté leeks until soft, about 8-10 minutes.

Add remaining ingredients and simmer for 20 minutes.

Remove from stove.

Basil-Garlic Oil *(Makes 1 cup)*

1   cup + 2 tablespoons **extra virgin olive oil**
8   cloves **garlic**
1   cup fresh **basil**, chopped

For Basil-Garlic Oil Heat 1 cup oil until hot.

Add garlic and remove from stove.

Allow to steep one hour.

Strain oil.

Steam basil lightly and squeeze moisture out of basil.

Place half of the basil into a blender with ¼ cup of the steeped oil, finely purée.

Strain into a storage container.

Repeat with the remaining basil and oil and strain into the same storage container.

Add the remaining 2 tablespoons of oil to the blender. Shake well and strain into the same storage container.

Refrigerate until ready to use.

Suggested Wine: Byron Pinot Noir 2001 Sierra Madre Vineyard

Grilled Jumbo Shrimp *with* Andouille Vinaigrette *and* Cheddar Cheese Grits Cake

24	jumbo **shrimp**, peeled and deveined, tail on
¼	cup **Mustard Marinade** (see recipe below)
4	cups **Mesclun (spring mix) greens**
8	**red teardrop tomatoes**
8	**yellow teardrop tomatoes**
1	cup **Creole Mustard Andouille Vinaigrette** (see opposite page)
8	pieces **Cheddar Cheese Grit Cake**, 2" x 2" squares (see recipe below)
4	teaspoons fresh **chives**, chopped

Mustard Marinade *(Makes 1 cup)*

⅓	cup **Dijon mustard**
1	cup **olive oil**
2	teaspoons **black pepper**
1	teaspoon **kosher salt**
2	teaspoons fresh **thyme**, finely chopped
1	teaspoon fresh **rosemary**, finely chopped
1	clove **garlic**, puréed with the olive oil

Cheddar Cheese Grits *(Makes 8 pieces)*

2	cups **water**
2	cups **milk**
4	teaspoons **garlic**, finely chopped
1	cup **white quick grits**
1	teaspoon **black pepper**
4	tablespoons fresh **chives**, finely chopped
1	cup **cheddar cheese**, shredded
½	cup **Tomato Basil Sauce** (see page 15)

Brush shrimp with Mustard Marinade on both sides and marinate overnight.

Grill jumbo shrimp and cook until done, about 6–8 minutes.

Warm greens and tomatoes slightly with ½ cup of Creole Mustard Andouille Vinaigrette.

Warm Cheddar Cheese Grit Cakes in oven and finish in broiler until golden.

Place one Cheddar Cheese Grit Cake on each serving plate.

Place ¼ of the greens and tomatoes on top of the Cheddar Cheese Grit Cake and place another grit cake on top of the greens.

Top with cooked jumbo shrimp and remaining greens and tomatoes.

Ladle remaining Creole Mustard Andouille Vinaigrette over top and sprinkle with chopped chives.

For Mustard Marinade Mix well.

For Cheddar Cheese Grits Combine water, milk and garlic in saucepan and cook until scalding.

Reduce to a simmer on low heat and add grits, cook for 6–8 minutes.

Remove from heat and add pepper, chives, cheese and Tomato Basil Sauce and mix well.

Pour into a 9 x 12-inch baking dish that has been brushed with butter.

Allow to cool until ready to use.

Creole Mustard Andouille Vinaigrette
(Makes 3 cups)

8	oz.	**Andouille sausage**, finely chopped
2	tablespoons	**red onion**, finely chopped
1	clove	**garlic**, finely chopped
1½	cups	**olive oil**
¼	cup	**balsamic vinegar**
¼	cup	**Zatarains Creole Mustard**
2	teaspoons	**sugar**
1	teaspoon	**salt**
½	teaspoon	**black pepper**

For Creole Mustard Andouille Vinaigrette Cook sausage in sauté pan on medium heat for 2 minutes.

Add red onion and garlic and sauté for 2 minutes until soft.

Add olive oil, balsamic vinegar and Zatarains Creole Mustard and mix well. Cook for an additional 2 minutes.

Stir in sugar, salt and black pepper. Mix well and remove from stove. Keep warm until ready to use.

Suggested Wine: Gainey 2001 Limited Selection Chardonnay Santa Cruz Valley

Pan Fried Soft Shelled Crabs *with* Pecan-Lemon Butter *in a* Ginger Cilantro Batter

8   pieces **soft shell crabs**,
      Hotel size, cleaned*
2   cups **milk**, for soaking
      all-purpose flour, for dusting
      Ginger Cilantro Batter
         (see page 20)
2   cups **vegetable oil**
2   cups **Pecan Wild Rice Pilaf**
         (see page 140)
1   cup **Pecan-Lemon Butter** melted
         (see recipe below)
6   sprigs **cilantro**, finely chopped

Pecan-Lemon Butter *(Makes 1 cup)*
½   lb. **butter** softened
2   tablespoons **pecan halves**,
      toasted, chopped
2   tablespoons fresh **parsley**, chopped
1   tablespoon fresh **lemon juice**

Soak cleaned soft shell crabs in milk for 1 hour.

Add oil to large sauté pan and heat.

Dust soft shell crabs in flour and then coat well in the Ginger Cilantro Batter.

Place in hot oil and cook on both sides until they are nice and crispy.

Place ½ cup Pecan Wild Rice Pilaf in center of each serving plate

Place 2 each of the soft shell crabs on top of Pecan Wild Rice Pilaf and pour ¼ cup Pecan-Lemon Butter over top of soft shell crabs.

Sprinkle with chopped cilantro.

Cleaning of soft shell crabs can be a bit squeamish, but the efforts outweigh that little bit of concern. Fresh soft shell crabs are available from May to July and this is a time to make an effort for these rich delicacies.

*Soft shells are graded by size and we think the Hotels are very good eating. Simple cleaning instructions follow: Using a pair of kitchen scissors, snip off the eyes and mouth in one piece.

Pull apart each side of the top shell and pull out and discard the gills.

Turn the crab over and pull off the little flap called the apron.

Clean under cold water.

For Pecan-Lemon Butter Whip butter in mixer.

Add all ingredients and mix well.

Refrigerate until ready to use.

Suggested Wine: Silverado Vineyards Sauvignon Blanc 2002 Napa Valley

Grilled Rainbow Trout *with* Pancetta Mustard Vinaigrette *and* Fried Leeks

4	8 oz. pieces **rainbow trout**, boned
¼	cup **olive oil**
2	teaspoons **sea salt**
2	cups **leeks**, finely julienned, 4" long, soak in water
	all-purpose flour, for dusting leeks
1	cup **Pancetta Mustard Vinaigrette**, warm (see recipe below)
4	teaspoons fresh **chives**, chopped

Pancetta Mustard Vinaigrette
(Makes 1 cup)

½	cup **pancetta**, chopped into ½" pieces
2	tablespoons fresh **lemon juice**
1	tablespoon **Dijon mustard**
1	tablespoon **balsamic vinegar**
⅔	cup **olive oil**
¼	cup fresh **chives**, chopped
½	teaspoon **salt**
½	teaspoon **black pepper**

Brush rainbow trout with olive oil and sprinkle with sea salt.

Place trout on hot grill and cook on both sides, about 3–4 minutes until done.

While fish is cooking, dust leeks in flour and fry until crispy.

Place trout on each serving plate. Ladle warm Pancetta Mustard Vinaigrette over top of trout.

Top with fried leeks and garnish with chopped chives.

For Pancetta Mustard Vinaigrette Place pancetta in large sauté pan and render well. Remove from oil with slotted spoon and set aside.

Add lemon juice, Dijon mustard and vinegar. Place in blender and blend well.

Slowly add olive oil to blender and emulsify well.

Remove and place in mixing bowl, add chives, salt, black pepper and cooked pancetta.

Mix well.

Keep at room temperature until ready to serve.

Suggested Wine: Snoqualmie Vineyards Chardonnay 2001 Washington

Seared Salmon Open Ravioli *with* Tomato Vinaigrette

4   4 oz. pieces **salmon**, skinned

4   teaspoons **Paul Prudhomme Cajun Seasoning**

8   pieces **pasta sheets**, 4" x 4" (see sources, page 192)

1   cup **Eggplant Caponata** (see page 110)

2   cups **Tomato Vinaigrette** (see recipe below)

4   teaspoons fresh **chives**, chopped

Tomato Vinaigrette

¾   cup **V-8 juice**

¾   cup **Tomato Basil Sauce** (see page 15)

3   tablespoons **extra virgin olive oil**

3   tablespoons **red wine vinegar**

2   tablespoons fresh **basil**

1   teaspoon **kosher salt**

¼   teaspoon **black pepper**

For Tomato Vinaigrette Combine V-8 juice, Tomato Basil Sauce, olive oil and vinegar in a saucepan and bring to a boil. Stir in the basil, salt and pepper; mix well. Remove from heat.

For Preparation of Ravioli Season salmon with Paul Prudhomme Cajun Seasonings and pan sear in a sauté pan with 2 tablespoons of oil and cook until crispy on both sides.

Cook pasta sheets in boiling water and drain.

Place 1 pasta square in each pasta bowl. Add ¼ cup hot Eggplant Caponata on top of pasta sheet. Place seared salmon on top of Eggplant Caponata. Place second pasta sheet on top of salmon.

Ladle ½ cup hot Tomato Vinaigrette over pasta.

Garnish with chopped chives.

Suggested Wine: Acacia Chardonnay 2002 Carneros

Grilled Florida Grouper *with* Macadamia Ginger Butter *and* Pineapple Salsa

4	8 oz. pieces **black grouper**, skin removed
½	cup **olive oil**
2	teaspoons **sea salt**
4	cups **Coconut-Curry Basmati Rice** (see page 140)
1	cup **Macadamia Ginger Butter** (see recipe below)
2	cups **Pineapple Salsa** (see recipe below)
4	cups steamed **snow peas**
4	teaspoons fresh **chives**, finely chopped

Macadamia Nut-Ginger Butter
(Makes 1 cup)

½	cup **butter**, softened
2	teaspoons **ginger**, grated
2	teaspoons **cilantro**, finely chopped
⅓	cup fresh **lime juice**
¼	teaspoon **salt**
⅛	teaspoon **white pepper**
¼	cup **macadamia nuts**, toasted and finely chopped

Pineapple Salsa *(Makes 2 cups)*

1	small **red onion**, finely chopped
1	tablespoon **jalapeño pepper**, seeded and finely chopped
2	tablespoons **ginger**, grated
¼	cup **orange juice**
1	cup fresh **pineapple**, peeled, chopped into ½" pieces
2	tablespoons fresh **mint**, finely chopped
2	tablespoons fresh **basil**, finely chopped
1	teaspoon **curry powder**
¼	cup **red bell pepper**, finely chopped

Brush grouper with olive oil and sprinkle with sea salt.

Place on grill at medium high heat.

Cook on both sides until done, about 8–10 minutes.

Place 1 cup Coconut Curry Basmati Rice in center of each serving plate and place grilled grouper on top.

Top grouper with 2 tablespoons Macadamia Ginger Butter and ¼ cup Pineapple Salsa.

Place 1 cup steamed snow peas next to Coconut Curry Basmati Rice and sprinkle chives over top of fish.

For Macadamia Nut-Ginger Butter Combine in food processor and mix very well.

Refrigerate until ready to use.

For Pineapple Salsa Mix all ingredients well and serve at room temperature.

Suggested Wine: Iron Horse 2002 T-Bar-T Viognier

Grilled Serrano Wrapped BBQ Shrimp

20	large jumbo **shrimp**, peeled, deveined, tail on
8	oz. **Serrano ham**, sliced very thinly
2	cups **Shrimp Marinade** (see opposite page)
2	cups **Shrimp BBQ Sauce** (see recipe below)
4	cups **Pecan Wild Rice Pilaf** (see page 140)
4	pieces fresh **herb** sprigs
4	**9" wooden skewers**

Spicy Shrimp BBQ Sauce
(Makes 2 cups)

1½	cups **The Grill's BBQ Sauce** (see page 185)
⅓	cup **dark molasses**
¼	cup **soy sauce**
2	tablespoons **brown sugar**
2	teaspoons **Dijon mustard**
2	**garlic** cloves, finely chopped
¼	cup fresh **lemon juice**
⅓	cup **Chicken Stock** (see page 16)
½	cup **water**
2	teaspoons **Tabasco sauce**
2	teaspoons **kosher salt**
4	teaspoons **Lea & Perrins**
¼	teaspoon **red pepper chili flakes**
1	**Poblano chili pepper**, seeded, chopped into ½" pieces

Wrap each shrimp with a slice of Serrano ham and place 5 shrimp on each 9" wooden skewer.

Pour Shrimp Marinade over shrimp and marinate for 6 hours or overnight.

Remove shrimp from marinade and brush with Shrimp BBQ Sauce.

Place shrimp on grill and cook on medium high heat on both sides until cooked, about 8–10 minutes. Baste shrimp while cooking.

Place Pecan Wild Rice Pilaf in center of each serving plate and remove shrimp from skewer and place around rice.

Drizzle remaining Shrimp BBQ Sauce over top of shrimp.

Garnish with herb sprig.

For Spicy Shrimp BBQ Sauce Combine all ingredients in mixing bowl and mix well.

Add to large saucepan and bring to a boil. Reduce heat and simmer until reduced by ½.

Allow to cool.

Purée in food processor.

For Shrimp Marinade Combine all ingredients in mixing bowl and then marinate shrimp well for 6 hours.

Suggested Wine: Cinnabar Sleepy Hollow Vineyard Chardonnay 2002

Marinade for Shrimp *(Makes 2 cups)*

¼ cup **Dijon mustard**
10 **garlic** cloves, crushed
5 sprigs fresh **rosemary**
5 sprigs fresh **thyme**
5 sprigs fresh **oregano**
1½ cups **olive oil**
½ teaspoon **black pepper**

Grilled Yellowtail Snapper *with* Poblano Peach Butter *and* Charred Jalapeño Vinaigrette

4	8 oz. pieces **yellowtail snapper**, skin removed
½	cup **olive oil**
2	teaspoons **sea salt**
½	cup **Poblano Peach Butter** (see recipe below)
4	portions **Fingerling Potatoes** (see page 143)
1	cup **Charred Jalapeño Vinaigrette** (see opposite page)
4	portions **Sautéed Spinach** (see page 145)
4	teaspoons fresh **chives**, finely chopped

Poblano Peach Butter
(Makes 2 cups)

1	tablespoon **olive oil**
1	**red pepper**, seeded, finely diced
2	**Poblano peppers**, seeded, finely diced
¼	cup **red onions**, finely diced
⅓	cup **red wine vinegar**
1	teaspoon **sugar**
¼	teaspoon **cayenne pepper**
1	cup **peaches**, peeled, chopped
1½	cups **butter**, softened

Brush snapper with olive oil and sprinkle with sea salt.

Place on grill at medium high heat and cook on both sides until done, about 5–7 minutes.

Place Fingerling Potatoes in center of each serving plate and place snapper on top of potatoes.

Top with 2 tablespoons Peach Poblano Butter and then drizzle ¼ cup Charred Jalapeño Vinaigrette over top of fish.

Place Sautéed Spinach next to fish and top with chopped chives.

For Poblano Peach Butter Heat oil in sauté pan.

Add red pepper, Poblano and red onion, sauté until peppers are soft.

Add vinegar, sugar and cayenne pepper. Simmer until liquid has evaporated, about 3–4 minutes. Allow to cool.

Process peaches and butter together in food processor, mixing well. Add cooled chili mixture and blend well.

Charred Jalapeño Vinaigrette
(Makes 2 cups)

2   tablespoons **olive oil**
2   **jalapeño peppers**, stems cut off
¼   cup **red onions**, finely chopped
2   **garlic** cloves, finely chopped
2   tablespoons **Dijon mustard**
2   tablespoons **red wine vinegar**
2   tablespoons **balsamic vinegar**
2   tablespoons **rice wine vinegar**
2   tablespoons **sesame oil**
4   tablespoons fresh **basil**,
          finely julienned
1   tablespoon **ancho chili powder**
2   teaspoons **kosher salt**
½   teaspoon **black pepper**
1   cup **extra virgin olive oil**

For Charred Jalapeño Vinaigrette   Heat olive oil in sauté pan.

Add whole jalapeño peppers and cook on all sides until skin is charred, let peppers cool.

Slice jalapeños thin, including seeds.

In large mixing bowl, combine remaining ingredients with the jalapeños and whisk in extra virgin olive oil slowly.

Suggested Wine: Château St. Jean Pinot Blanc 2001 Robert Young Vineyard

Grilled Sea Bass *with* Eggplant Caponata *and* Roasted Tomato-Kalamata Vinaigrette

4	8 oz. pieces **sea bass**, skin removed
¼	cup **olive oil**
2	teaspoons **sea salt**
4	cups **Garlic Olive Mashers** (see page 141)
1	cup **Roasted Tomato and Kalamata Vinaigrette**, warm (see opposite page)
½	cup **Eggplant Caponata** (see recipe below)
4	teaspoons fresh **chives**, chopped

Eggplant Caponata *(Makes 1 cup)*

½	cup **eggplant**, chopped into ¼" pieces
¼	teaspoon **kosher salt**
3	tablespoons **olive oil**
¼	cup **onion**, chopped into ¼" pieces
¼	cup **celery**, chopped into ¼" pieces
1	teaspoon **red wine vinegar**
⅛	teaspoon **white pepper**
2	tablespoons **sugar**
½	cup **crushed tomatoes**
¼	cup **red pepper**, roasted, chopped into ¼" pieces
2	tablespoons **black oil cured olives**, chopped
2	teaspoons **capers**, rinsed, chopped
½	**anchovy**, finely chopped

Brush sea bass with olive oil and sprinkle with sea salt.

Place fish on hot grill and cook on both sides for about 5–6 minutes until done.

Place 1 cup Garlic Olive Mashers in center of each serving plate and place sea bass on top of mashers.

Ladle ¼ cup Roasted Tomato Kalamata Vinaigrette over top of fish.

Place 2 tablespoons Eggplant Caponata on top of fish.

Garnish with chopped chives.

For Eggplant Caponata Toss eggplant with salt and let stand for one hour at room temperature.

Rinse eggplant with cold water. Squeeze to remove excess liquid.

Heat oil in saucepan and sauté eggplant until browned, about 5–6 minutes.

Add 3 tablespoons olive oil to pan and add onion and celery. Cook until soft.

Add vinegar, white pepper and sugar and cook until vinegar is reduced to a glaze, about 5–8 minutes.

Add tomatoes and cook until thickened, about 10 minutes.

Add tomatoes to bowl with eggplant and fold in peppers, olives, capers and anchovies.

For Roasted Tomato and Kalamata Vinaigrette Place all ingredients in mixing bowl and combine well. Place in refrigerator until ready to use.

Suggested Wine: Simi Sauvignon Blanc 2002 Sonoma

Roasted Tomato and Kalamata
Vinaigrette *(Makes 2 cups)*

1	lb. **tomatoes**, roasted and chopped	
¼	cup **extra virgin olive oil**	
½	cup **white wine vinegar**	
2	tablespoons fresh **basil**, julienned	
¼	cup **red onions**, finely chopped	
¼	cup **Bloody Mary Mix**	
½	cup **Tomato Basil Sauce** (see page 15)	
¼	cup **Kalamata olives**, chopped	
1	**anchovy**, chopped	
½	teaspoon **capers**, chopped	
½	teaspoon fresh **lemon juice**	
1	**garlic** clove, roasted and finely chopped	

Miso Glazed Ahi Tuna

4	6 oz. pieces **ahi tuna**, 1" thick
1	cup **Miso Glaze Marinade** (see opposite page)
2	cups **Asian Vegetable Mix** (see recipe below)
2	cups **Miso Broth** (see recipe below)
	Lobster Mashers (see page 151)
4	tablespoons **Wasabi Butter** (see opposite page)
16	sprigs **cilantro**

Asian Vegetable Mix *(Serves 4)*

½	cup **pea pods**, finely julienned
½	cup **daikon radish**, finely julienned
½	cup **carrots**, finely julienned
½	cup **shitake mushrooms**, thinly sliced

Miso Broth *(Makes 2 cups)*

2	cups **Chicken Stock** (see page 16)
1	tablespoon **Kikkoman Teriyaki Sauce**
4	teaspoons **mirin**
4	teaspoons **rice wine vinegar**
¼	teaspoon **garlic**, chopped
¼	teaspoon **ginger purée**
½	teaspoon **sugar**
½	teaspoon **sesame oil**

Preheat oven to 400°.

Marinate tuna with ½ cup of Miso Glaze Marinade for 3–4 hours.

Place tuna on grill on medium high heat and cook 3–4 minutes on each side until rare to medium rare.

Brush tuna with remaining Miso Glaze Marinade while cooking.

While you are cooking tuna place Asian Vegetable Mix in preheated oven with Miso Broth and cook until warm.

Place 1 cup Lobster Mashers in center of each serving bowl.

Pour ½ cup hot Miso Broth and ½ cup Asian Vegeatable Mix in serving bowl around Lobster Mashers.

Place tuna on top of Lobster Mashers.

Drizzle tuna with softened Wasabi Butter.

Garnish with cilantro sprigs.

For Asian Vegetable Mix Combine all ingredients and refrigerate until ready to use.

For Miso Broth Whisk together in mixing bowl.

Refrigerate until ready to use.

Miso Glaze Marinade

(Makes 1 cup)

¼	cup	**Kikkoman Teriyaki Sauce**
⅓	cup	**miso**
2	tablespoons	**brown sugar**
½	teaspoon	**ginger**, grated
½	teaspoon	**ginger**, finely chopped
¼	cup	**sake**
¼	cup	**mirin**

Wasabi Butter

½	cup	**butter**
1	tablespoon	**wasabi powder**

For Miso Glaze Marinade Heat all ingredients in saucepan over low heat. Mix well until combined.

Allow to cool.

For Wasabi Butter Place butter in mixer. Whip until soft.

Add wasabi powder and mix well.

Refrigerate until ready to use.

Suggested Wine: Rodney Strong 2001 Reserve Chardonnay Chalk Hill

Grilled Catfish *with* Black Bean-Corn Salsa

4	6 oz. pieces **catfish fillets**, trimmed
¼	cup **olive oil**
4	tablespoons **Paul Prudhomme Cajun Seasoning**
4	tablespoons **Roasted Garlic Butter**, melted
2	cups **Whipped Sweet Potatoes**, mashed (see page 148)
1	cup **Black Bean-Corn Salsa** (see recipe below)
4	teaspoons fresh **chives**, finely chopped

Black Bean & Roasted Corn Salsa

(Makes 2 cups)

1	**ear fresh corn**, grilled
1	tablespoon **butter**, melted
1½	cups **black beans**, cooked
¼	cup **red bell pepper**, finely chopped
2	tablespoons **green onion**, thinly sliced
2	tablespoons **red onion**, finely chopped
1	teaspoon **cilantro**
1	teaspoon fresh **lime juice**
1	teaspoon **olive oil**
1	**garlic** clove, roasted, finely chopped
¼	cup **beefsteak tomato**, chopped into ½" pieces
¼	teaspoon **cumin**
1	teaspoon fresh **basil**, finely chopped

Brush catfish with olive oil and dust with Paul Prudhomme Cajun Seasoning.

Place on grill and cook on both sides about 3–4 minutes until cooked.

Place Whipped Sweet Potato Mashers in center of each serving plate.

Brush catfish with melted Roasted Garlic Butter and place on Whipped Sweet Potato Mashers.

Top catfish with ¼ cup Black Bean and Roasted Corn Salsa.

Garnish with chopped chives.

For Black Bean & Roasted Corn Salsa Brush corn with butter and place on grill. Cook on all sides until golden brown. Set aside until ready to take off cob.

Take corn off the cob and place in mixing bowl. Combine with all other ingredients and mix well.

Suggested Wine: Carmenet 2002 Chardonnay

Grilled Atlantic Salmon *with* Balsamic Honey Glaze *and* Fresh Three Bean Salad

4   8 oz. pieces **salmon fillets**,
       skin removed
4   tablespoons **olive oil**
2   teaspoons **sea salt**
½   cup **Balsamic Honey Glaze**
       (see recipe below)
4   cups **Fresh Three Bean Salad**
       (see recipe below)
4   teaspoons fresh **tarragon**,
       finely chopped

Balsamic-Honey Glaze *(Makes ½ cup)*
2   tablespoons **olive oil**
10   cloves **garlic**, finely chopped
2   tablespoons **honey**
2   tablespoons **Dijon mustard**
¼   cup **balsamic vinegar**
1   teaspoon **salt**
1   teaspoon **black pepper**
2   tablespoons fresh **basil**, julienned

Fresh Three Bean Salad *(Serves 4)*
1   cup **green beans**, steamed
1   cup **yellow wax beans**, steamed
1   cup **navy beans**, cooked
1   cup **spinach**, cleaned
4   tablespoons **green onions**,
       thinly sliced
2   tablespoons fresh **tarragon**,
       finely chopped
¼   cup **rice wine vinegar**
2   tablespoons **sugar**
½   cup **extra virgin olive oil**

Brush salmon with olive oil and sprinkle with sea salt.

Place on grill on medium high heat and cook on both sides, about 4–5 minutes per side.

Brush with Balsamic Honey Glaze while cooking.

Place 1 cup warm Fresh Three Bean Salad on each serving plate.

Place salmon on top of warm Fresh Three Bean Salad and drizzle remaining Balsamic Honey Glaze over top of salmon.

Garnish with chopped tarragon.

For Balsamic-Honey Glaze Heat olive oil in saucepan.

Add garlic and lightly sauté.

Add honey, mustard, balsamic vinegar, salt and pepper, stir until well combined.

Simmer for 3–4 minutes until slightly thickened, remove from stove.

Stir in julienned basil and mix well.

For Fresh Three Bean Salad Combine tarragon, vinegar, sugar and olive oil in mixing bowl.

Toss with all beans and vegetables and place in large sauté pan.

Warm lightly.

Suggested Wine: Sokol Blosser Pinot Noir 2001 Willamette Valley

Grilled Halibut *with* Chimichurri Sauce *and* Yellow Tomato Concasse

4	8 oz. pieces **halibut fillets**, skin removed
¼	cup **olive oil**
2	teaspoons **sea salt**
4	pieces **Goat Cheese Potato Leek Cakes** (see page 143)
1	cup **Chimichurri Sauce** (see recipe below)
1	cup **Yellow Tomato Concasse** (see recipe below)
4	teaspoons fresh **chives**, chopped

Chimichurri Sauce *(Makes 1 cup)*

3	**garlic** cloves, finely chopped
2	basil **leaves**, finely chopped
1	**jalapeño pepper**, finely chopped
1½	teaspoons **sea salt**
½	cup fresh **parsley**, finely chopped
2	tablespoons fresh **oregano**, finely chopped
2	tablespoons **white vinegar**
3	tablespoons **extra virgin olive oil**

Yellow Tomato Concasse

(Makes 1½ cups)

1	cup **beefsteak yellow tomatoes**, seeded, chopped into small pieces
3	tablespoons **extra virgin olive oil**
¼	teaspoon **black pepper**
2	teaspoons **salt**
1	tablespoon fresh **chives**, finely chopped

Brush halibut with olive oil and sprinkle with sea salt.

Place fish on hot grill and cook on both sides for 4–5 minutes until done.

Heat Goat Cheese Potato Leek Cakes in oven until golden and hot.

Place one Goat Cheese Potato Leek Cake in center of each serving plate and place halibut on top of it.

Top halibut with ¼ cup Chimichurri Sauce then ¼ cup Yellow Tomato Concasse.

Top with chopped chives.

For Chimichurri Sauce Mix all ingredients together well.

For Yellow Tomato Concasse Mix all ingredients in a mixing bowl.

Keep at room temperature until ready to use.

Suggested Wine: King Estate Pinot Gris 2002 Oregon

Shrimp *and* Scallops Fettuccine Verde

1	lb. **spinach fettuccine noodles** (see sources, page 192)
1	cup **Olive Oil Garlic & Herb Sauce** (see page 14)
16	large **shrimp**, tail off, peeled and deveined
12	medium **scallops**
½	cup **Tomato Basil Sauce** (see page 15)
½	cup **Roasted Garlic Butter** (see page 14)
4	tablespoons fresh **basil**, finely julienned
2	cups **Egg-Cream Mixture** (see recipe below)
1	cup **goat cheese**
4	tablespoons **sun dried tomatoes**

Egg-Cream Mixture

2	**egg yolks**
2	cups **heavy cream**

Cook fettuccine noodles until al dente.

Place Olive Oil Garlic & Herb Sauce in sauté pan and heat.

Add shrimp and scallops and cook for one minute. Add Tomato Basil Sauce, Roasted Garlic Butter and basil. Cook until shrimp and scallops are done.

Add Egg-Cream Mixture and goat cheese. Cook until it bubbles, do not break goat cheese up.

Add cooked fettuccine noodles and toss well.

Place noodles on each serving plate and pour sauce over top.

Garnish with sun dried tomatoes.

For Egg-Cream Mixture Whisk together egg yolks and heavy cream.

Suggested Wine: Qupe Ibarra Young Viognier 2001

Seafood Diablo Pasta

1   cup **Red Bell Pepper Butter**
        (see page 16)
½   lb. **salmon**, skinned, 1" cubed pieces
12   **scallops**, medium size
8   **shrimp**, large, peeled, deveined,
        tail off
½   lb. **lobster meat**, chopped
4   cups **Diablo Sauce** (see page 70)
1   lb. **red pepper linguine**, cooked
        (see sources, page 192)
2   sautéed **Poblano Peppers**
        (see recipe below)

Poblano Peppers *(Serves 4)*
2   tablespoons **olive oil**
2   **Poblano peppers**, julienned into
        ½" pieces

Cook linguine until al dente.

Place Red bell Pepper Butter and seafood in a sauté pan and cook until done.

Add Diablo Sauce into pan with seafood and heat.

Add cooked linguine and mix well.

Place pasta on serving plate and garnish with sautéed peppers.

For Poblano Peppers Place olive oil into sauté pan and heat. Add peppers and cook until golden brown. Reserve until ready to use.

Suggested Wine: Cambria Pinot Noir 2002 Julias Vineyard

Olive Oil Poached Halibut

2   cups **extra virgin olive oil**
1   cup **water**
1   cup **Roasted Garlic Butter** (see page 14)
4   6 oz. pieces **halibut**, skinned
4   portions **Spinach**, **Figs Chanterelles**
        and **Prosciutto** (see page 146)
2   cups **Fingerling Potatoes**
        (see page 143)
4   tablespoons **Lemon Garlic Aioli**
        (see page 80)
4   teaspoons fresh **chives**, finely chopped

Add extra virgin olive oil, water and Roasted Garlic Butter in large sauté pan and heat.

Add halibut, cover and cook on medium high heat until halibut is tender, about 10–12 minutes.

Place Spinach, Figs, Chanterelles and Prosciutto mixture in center of each serving plate.

Place Fingerling Potatoes on top of spinach.

Place halibut on top of Fingerling Potatoes.

Drizzle Lemon Garlic Aioli over top of halibut.

Garnish with chopped chives.

Suggested Wine: Trefethen Chardonnay 2002 Napa Valley

Meat & Poultry

You will be surprised to see a recipe for a Roasted Vegetable Plate and deluxe Mac & Cheese nestled in with the chicken and meat recipes. I just wanted to have some fun! I have chosen some different cuts of meat, accompanied by great sauces and beautiful presentations. After all, they are the centerpieces of your meal. They may be a bit challenging, but oh so good!

Roasted Vegetable Plate

2   cups **Fingerling Potatoes** (see page 143)

12   **Roasted Asparagus spears**
        (see roasting instructions)

4   portions **Parmesan Custard**, warm
        (see page 38)

2   cups **Sautéed Spinach** (see page 145)

2   **Roasted Portobello Mushrooms**,
        sliced (see roasting instructions)

1   lb. **Honey Glazed Carrots**
        (see page 148)

½   lb. sautéed **French beans**

½   lb. sautéed **yellow wax beans**

2   tablespoons **butter**, melted,
        for sautéing beans

Follow proper cooking procedures for the ingredients and place on serving platter.

Start with Roasted Portobello Mushrooms, then Sautéed Spinach across from the Roasted Portobello Mushrooms.

Place Fingerling Potatoes in center of plate.

Place Parmesan Custard next to Fingerling Potatoes.

Place sautéed beans and Roasted Asparagus next to Roasted Portobello Mushrooms.

Place Honey Glazed Carrots next to Roasted Portobello Mushrooms.

I find that tossing fresh vegetables with extra virgin olive oil and fine sea salt, placing them in an oven at 400° and cooking them until tender really brings the flavors out in each vegetable. Try this recipe. You could also add a little spice with a sprinkling of ground fennel.

Suggested Wine: Quivira Sauvignon Blanc 2002 Fig Tree Vineyard, Dry Creek Valley

Hazelnut Crusted Lamb Ribeye

4   12–14 oz. **lamb racks**, bones removed
1   cup **Lamb Marinade**
        (see recipe below)
½   cup **olive oil**
4   tablespoons **Dijon mustard**
     Hazelnut Bread Crumbs
        (see opposite page)
4   cups **orzo pasta**, cooked
1   cup **shitake mushrooms**,
        sautéed in butter
½   cup **radicchio**, julienned
1   cup **Pomegranate Honey Mint Sauce**
        (see opposite page)
4   fresh **herb** sprigs

Lamb Marinade
¾   cup **olive oil**
2   tablespoons fresh **rosemary,**
        finely chopped
4   **garlic** cloves, finely chopped
2   tablespoons **orange juice**
¼   teaspoon **black pepper**

For Lamb Marinade Mix all ingredients together.

Preparation of Lamb Ribeye Preheat oven to 400°.

Remove lamb loin from rack, leaving fat cap on.

Marinate lamb ribeye for 2 hours.

Place oil in large sauté pan and heat. Place marinated lamb in oil and pan sear until golden in color on both sides. Remove and allow to cool before proceeding to next step.

Brush lamb lightly with Dijon mustard and coat well with Hazelnut Bread Crumbs.

Place lamb ribeye in oven and cook until desired doneness.

Place orzo, shitake mushrooms and radicchio in broiler and warm. Place in center of serving platter.

Pour ¼ cup Pomegranate Honey Mint Sauce next to orzo on serving dish and place sliced lamb ribeye on top of sauce.

Garnish with fresh herb sprig.

For Pomegranate Honey Mint Sauce Place Lamb Jus and orange juice in saucepan and bring to a boil over medium heat.

Add ginger, honey, pomegranate molasses, vinegar, mint, thyme and sesame oil. Cook until mixture is reduced and syrupy, about 20 minutes.

Add mustard and butter and mix well. Remove from stove until ready to use.

For Hazelnut Bread Crumbs Place all ingredients in food processor and pulse until well combined.

Suggested Wine: Cinnabar Merlot 2001 Paso Robles

Pomegranate Honey Mint Sauce
(Makes 1 cup)

1	cup **Lamb Jus** (see page 19)
3	tablespoons **orange juice**
2	teaspoons **ginger**, grated
⅓	cup **honey**
1	teaspoon **pomegranate molasses** (see sources, page 192)
2	tablespoons **balsamic vinegar**
1	teaspoon fresh **thyme**, finely chopped
2	tablespoons fresh **mint**, finely chopped
½	teaspoon **sesame oil**
2	teaspoons **Dijon mustard**
2	tablespoons **butter**

Hazelnut Bread Crumbs *(Makes 1½ cups)*

1	cup **bread crumbs**, toasted
⅓	cup peeled **hazelnuts**, toasted
1	**shallot**
3	**garlic** cloves, roasted
1	tablespoon **orange zest**
2	tablespoons **peanut oil**
2	tablespoons fresh **parsley**, chopped
1	tablespoon fresh **mint**, finely chopped
1	teaspoon fresh **thyme**, finely chopped

Roasted Pork Rack *with* Cider Pepper Glaze

1	**8-bone pork rack**, about 4–5 lbs.
4	cups **Whipped Sweet Potatoes** (see page 148)
1	cup **Cider Pepper Glaze** (see recipe below)
1½	cups **yellow wax beans**, trimmed and blanched
1½	cups **French beans**, trimmed and blanched
4	fresh **herb** sprigs
¼	cup **butter**, melted, for beans

Pork Rack Cure Preparation
(Makes enough for one, 8-bone pork rack, about 4–5 lbs.)

½	cup **maple syrup**
2	cups **water**
2	tablespoons **sugar**
2	tablespoons **brown sugar**
2	tablespoons **kosher salt**
1	**bay leaf**
4	**juniper berries**, crushed
2	sprigs fresh **thyme**

Cider Pepper Glaze *(Makes 2 cups)*

1½	quarts **apple cider**
2	**Granny Smith apples**, peeled, chopped into ½" pieces
¼	cup **cider vinegar**
¼	cup **honey**
1	tablespoon **garlic**, finely chopped
3	sprigs fresh **thyme**
1	tablespoon **mustard seeds**, crushed
10	**juniper berries**, crushed
1	tablespoon **Peppercorn Melange Mix**, crushed

For Pork Rack Preheat oven to 450°.

Trim excess fat from pork and bones.

Score pork in a crisscross fashion without cutting into the flesh.

Submerge pork rack into pork curing water (see preparation) for 24 hours.

Remove, rinse and pat dry. Place in oven for 40-45 minutes until cooked through.

Allow to rest.

Place Whipped Sweet Potatoes in center of serving platter.

Slice pork rack into 1" chops and place rib chop leaning on Whipped Sweet Potatoes.

Ladle hot Cider Pepper Glaze over top of rib chop.

Steam, blanch and toss French beans and yellow wax beans with melted butter.

Place beans next to Whipped Sweet Potatoes. Garnish with fresh herb sprig.

For Cider Pepper Glaze Combine apple cider, apples, vinegar, honey, garlic, thyme, mustard seeds and juniper berries in stainless steel saucepan. Bring to a boil over high heat.

Lower heat to a simmer for 25 minutes. Strain and add peppercorns. Cook over high heat for 20 minutes and reduce to 2 cups.

Suggested Wine: Girard Zinfandel 2001 Napa Valley

Return to the Common Grill

Oven Roasted Chicken Breasts

4	6 oz. pieces **boneless chicken breast**
¼	cup per breast **Goat Cheese Pancetta Stuffing** (see opposite page)
½	cup **Herb Marinade** (see page 22)
2	cups **White Cheddar Mashers** (see page 151)
1	lb. **Honey Glazed Carrots** (see page 148)
1	cup **Roasted Lemon and Rosemary Sauce** (see recipe below)
4	sprigs fresh **herb garnish**

Roasted Lemon and Rosemary Sauce
(Makes 2 cups)

2	tablespoons **extra virgin olive oil**
3	tablespoons **garlic**, roasted and minced
⅔	cup **Roasted Lemon Juice** (see page 58)
4	tablespoons fresh **rosemary**, minced
3	tablespoons fresh **parsley**, minced
2½	cups **Brown Chicken Stock** (double strength) (see page 17)
3	tablespoons **butter**, softened
3	tablespoons **flour**
1	teaspoon cracked **black pepper**

Preheat oven to 400°.

Pound chicken breasts to ¼" thickness.

Place Goat Cheese Pancetta Stuffing in center and roll chicken breast to enclose stuffing.

Brush with Herb Marinade and allow to marinate 1 hour.

Place in oven for 30–45 minutes until cooked through.

Place White Cheddar Mashers in center of serving platter.

Place hot Honey Glazed Carrots next to White Cheddar Mashers.

Slice chicken breast and place leaning on White Cheddar Mashers.

Ladle hot Roasted Lemon and Rosemary Sauce over top of chicken breasts.

Garnish with fresh herb sprig.

For Roasted Lemon and Rosemary Sauce Heat oil in saucepan.

Add garlic and sauté lightly.

Add Roasted Lemon Juice, rosemary and parsley. Cook for 2 minutes.

Add Brown Chicken Stock and bring to a boil.

Combine butter and flour together to form a paste and add to stock.

Add cracked pepper.

Continue to cook and allow to thicken.

Remove from stove.

Goat Cheese Pancetta Stuffing

(Makes enough for 6 chicken breasts)

1	cup **goat cheese**
2	tablespoons **sun-dried tomatoes**, finely chopped
½	cup **pancetta,** cooked, chopped into ½" pieces
½	cup **mozzarella cheese**, shredded
½	cup **ricotta cheese**, shredded
2	tablespoons **Romano cheese**, grated
2	tablespoons fresh **basil**, finely julienned

For Goat Cheese Pancetta Stuffing Mix all ingredients in mixing bowl and refrigerate until ready to use.

Suggested Wine: Artesa Pinot Noir 2001 Russian River Valley

Grilled Chicken Breasts *with* Kahlua Espresso BBQ Sauce

4   8 oz. **chicken breasts**, boneless with
    wing joint attached
2   cups **Kahlua Espresso BBQ Sauce**
    (see page 185)
1   lb. **Honey Glazed Carrots**
    (see page 148)
2   cups **Pecan Wild Rice Pilaf**
    (see page 140)
4   fresh **herb** sprigs

Preheat oven to 400°.

Marinate chicken breasts in 1 cup of Kahlua Espresso BBQ Sauce for 1 hour.

Place chicken in oven and cook for 15–20 minutes.

Place chicken on grill and begin to baste with remaining sauce. Be careful not to burn chicken.

Place chicken on serving plate and ladle remaining sauce over top of chicken.

Serve with Pecan Wild Rice Pilaf, Honey Glazed Carrots and garnish with an herb sprig.

Suggested Wine: Edna Valley Pinot Noir 2002 Paragon Vineyards

Return to the Common Grill

Deluxe Mac *and* Cheese

4	cups **penne pasta**, cooked
2	tablespoons **butter**
¼	cup **onion**
2	tablespoons **all-purpose flour**
1½	cups **milk**, scalded
	pinch **kosher salt**
	pinch **black pepper**
	pinch **nutmeg**
1	cup **Gorgonzola cheese**
⅓	cup **mozzarella cheese**
⅓	cup **smoked provolone cheese**
⅓	cup **Romano cheese**
¼	cup fresh **basil**, chopped
2	tablespoons fresh **parsley**, chopped
½	cup **ricotta**, crumbled
¼	cup **Parmesan cheese**, grated

Lemon Cheese Bread Crumb Topping

½	cup **Lemon Bread Crumbs** (see recipe below)
½	cup **Parmesan cheese**

Lemon Bread Crumbs

1	cup homemade **croutons**, coarsely crushed
1	tablespoon fresh **parsley**, finely chopped
1	tablespoon **lemon zest**, grated
2	tablespoons **olive oil**

Preheat oven to 350°.

Cook pasta and allow to cool.

Melt butter in saucepan.

Add onion and cook until soft.

Add flour and mix well.

Add milk, salt, black pepper and nutmeg and bring to a simmer over low heat, about 10 minutes.

Add herbs and cheeses. Mix well.

Add cooked pasta and mix well.

Place pasta into individual round au gratin dishes or 9 x 12-inch baking dish.

Top with Lemon Cheese Bread Crumb topping.

Bake in oven for 25–30 minutes until golden.

For Lemon Cheese Bread Crumb Topping Mix together well.

For Lemon Bread Crumbs Combine all ingredients and mix well.

Suggested Wine: Handley Cellars Pinot Gris 2002 Anderson Valley

Grilled Ribeye Steak *with* Blue Cheese Walnut Butter *and* Portobello Fries

4   4" **portobello mushroom** caps

1   cup **buttermilk**, for soaking
mushrooms

     all-purpose flour, for dusting
mushrooms

4   10 oz. portions **ribeye steak**

1   cup **Blue Cheese Walnut Butter**, room
temperature (see recipe below)

16   jumbo **asparagus spears**, trimmed,
grilled

4   fresh **herb** sprigs

Blue Cheese Walnut Butter
(Makes 2 cups)

½   lb. **butter**, softened

½   lb. **Maytag Blue cheese**, crumbled

1   tablespoon fresh **parsley**,
finely chopped

1   teaspoon fresh **rosemary**,
finely chopped

¼   cup **walnuts**, toasted, finely chopped

2   tablespoons **garlic**, roasted,
finely chopped

2   teaspoons **kosher salt**

½   teaspoon **black pepper**

Cut portobello mushrooms into ½" strips and soak in buttermilk for 30 minutes.

Dust mushroom slices in flour and place in fryer. Cook until crispy, about 5 minutes.

Grill ribeyes until desired doneness.

Place steaks on serving plate. Top with Blue Cheese Walnut Butter and place mushrooms on top of butter.

Place grilled asparagus next to steaks.

Garnish with fresh herb sprig.

For Blue Cheese Walnut Butter Soften butter in mixer.

Add all ingredients and mix well.

Keep chilled.

Suggested Wine: Merryvale Starmont Cabernet Sauvignon 2001 Napa Valley

Asian BBQ Pork Ribs

4   baby back ribs, 1½ lbs. each
4   teaspoons black & toasted white
      sesame seeds
1   cup Pickled Cucumber Salad
      (see recipe below)
4   teaspoons fresh chives, chopped
2   cups Asian BBQ Sauce
      (see recipe below)
      Rib Marinade, full recipe
      (see opposite page)

Pickled Cucumber Salad *(Serves 4)*
2   seedless cucumbers, peeled,
      thinly sliced
2   tablespoons Kikkoman Teriyaki sauce
2   tablespoons rice wine vinegar
2   teaspoons ginger, grated
2   teaspoons garlic, finely chopped
4   teaspoons sugar
4   teaspoons fresh basil, finely julienned
2   teaspoons jalapeño, finely chopped

Asian BBQ Sauce *(Makes 2 cups)*
1   cup white vinegar
2   cups Kikkoman Teriyaki sauce
¼   cup ginger, grated
¾   cup dark brown sugar
½   cup green onions, finely chopped
½   cup ketchup

Place 4 rib racks in roasting pan.

Pour Rib Marinade over top of ribs and marinate for 24 hours, covered.

Preheat oven to 300°.

Place aluminum foil over marinated ribs and place in oven.

After 1 hour rotate ribs and baste with marinade. Cover and place back in oven.

After 1 hour rotate ribs again and baste with marinade. Cover and place back in oven.

After ½ hour ladle 1 cup of Asian BBQ Sauce over ribs. Cover and place back in oven.

After 15 minutes remove cover and finish cooking for 15 more minutes.

Remove from oven and allow to cool.

For Pickled Cucumber Salad Mix all ingredients together.

For Asian BBQ Sauce Bring all ingredients (except green onions) to a boil in a saucepan.

Reduce heat to low and simmer for 30–45 minutes, until reduced by ½ and is thickened.

Add green onions, mix well and remove from stove.

Refrigerate until ready to use.

Rib Marinade

(Makes enough for four, 1½ lb. rib racks)

⅓	cup	**orange juice**
2	teaspoons	**orange zest**
2	cloves	**garlic,** finely chopped
2½	tablespoons	**ginger,** grated
⅓	cup	**molasses**
⅔	cup	**mirin**
2½	tablespoons	**Kikkoman Teriyaki sauce**
½	cup	**rice vinegar**
¼	cup	**olive oil**
1	teaspoon	**white pepper**

Preparation for serving Cut ribs into individual pieces.

Ladle 1 cup Asian BBQ Sauce over rib pieces and place in 450° oven and cook until hot, about 5–6 minutes.

Place Pickled Cucumber Salad on serving plate on the side.

Stack rib pieces like "Lincoln Logs" on serving plate. Pour sauce over top of ribs.

Top with black and white sesame seeds.

Sprinkle chopped chives over top of Pickled Cucumber Salad.

For Rib Marinade Mix together well.

Suggested Wine: Miner Merlot 2001 Oakville Ranch

Roasted Veal "Osso Bucco"

4	**veal shanks**, 16 oz. each, 2" thick
3	tablespoons **extra virgin olive oil**
½	cup **butter**
4	oz. **pancetta**, chopped
6	cloves **garlic**, finely chopped
½	cup **Spanish onions**, chopped into 1" pieces
½	cup **carrots**, chopped into 1" pieces
½	cup **celery**, chopped into 1" pieces
1	teaspoon fresh **basil**, finely chopped
1	teaspoon fresh **oregano**, finely chopped
2	pieces 3" **orange peel**
2	pieces 3" **lemon peel**
2	cups **crushed tomatoes**
1½	cups **Chicken Stock** (see page 16)
⅓	cup **white wine**

Lemon Gremolata

2	cloves **garlic**, finely chopped
¼	cup fresh **parsley**, finely chopped
	lemon zest of 2 lemons

4 Servings

4	pieces **veal shank**
4	cups **Veal Jus** (see page 20)
4	cups **Basil Mashers** (see page 152)
16	**asparagus spears**, roasted
4	tablespoons **Lemon Gremolata** (see recipe above)

For Veal Shanks Preheat oven to 300°.

Brush shanks with oil and grill on each side for 5 minutes. Set aside.

Melt butter in large, heavy bottomed saucepan. Add pancetta and cook for 2–3 minutes.

Add garlic, onion, carrots, and celery and sauté until onions are translucent.

Add basil and oregano and mix well.

Add veal shanks and the remaining ingredients.

Bring liquid to a boil and reduce to a simmer, cover and place in oven for 2½ hours.

Remove cover and bake for 30 minutes until shanks are cooked well.

Remove veal shanks from Veal Jus and place on top of Basil Mashers.

Pour 1 cup vegetable garniture and Veal Jus on top of each Osso Bucco.

Serve with roasted asparagus and top with Lemon Gremolata.

For Lemon Gremolata Combine all ingredients together and mix well.

Suggested Wine: Zaca Mesa Syrah Santa Ynez 2000

Sides

When serving guests for a dinner party, great side dishes compliment anything you do. Whether the honey roasted carrots are positioned across from the fish, or your mashers are settled gently under your beef, the stimulation of eye and palate will enhance the presentation. Of course, the aroma of it all will invite your guests right into the dining room.

Orzo, Lobster *and* Radicchio

¼	cup	**olive oil**
2		**garlic** cloves, finely chopped
½	cup	**crimini mushrooms**, thinly sliced
2	cups	**orzo pasta**, cooked
1	cup	**lobster meat**, chopped in large pieces
½	cup	**radicchio**, finely julienned
½	teaspoon	**kosher salt**

Heat oil in saucepan on medium heat.

Add garlic and cook until soft.

Add mushrooms, lobster meat, radicchio, orzo pasta and salt tossing well after each addition.

Heat until warmed throughout.

We use this with the Parmesan Crusted Whitefish recipe, but this would be a great side dish for any entrée.

Makes 4 cups

Couscous Jambalaya

8	oz.	**shrimp**, large, peeled, deveined, tail off
4	teaspoons	**Paul Prudhomme Cajun Seasoning**
½	cup	**olive oil**
4	oz.	**Andouille sausage**, chopped into ½" pieces
½	cup	**red onions**, chopped into ½" pieces
½	cup	**red peppers**, chopped into ½" pieces
3		**garlic** cloves, finely chopped
½	cup	**plum tomatoes**, chopped into ½" pieces
1½	cups	**Chicken Stock** (see page 16)
1	cup	**couscous**

Mix together shrimp and Paul Prudhomme Cajun Seasoning.

Sauté shrimp lightly in olive oil.

Add Andouille sausage, red onion, red peppers and garlic. Cook for 2 minutes.

Stir in tomatoes and Chicken Stock. Bring to a boil.

Add couscous.

Turn off heat. Cover and let sit for 5–8 minutes.

This is really good with grilled pork or chicken breast.

Makes 4 cups

Pecan Wild Rice Pilaf

1½	lbs. **Rice Pilaf** (entire recipe) (see page 140)
¼	cup **wild rice**, raw, pre-soaked
1	cup **Chicken Stock** (see page 16)
¼	cup **pecan halves**, chopped in large pieces
3	tablespoons **orange zest**
¼	cup **orange juice**
1	teaspoon **black pepper**, coarse
2	tablespoons **mint leaves**, finely chopped

Cook wild rice with 1 cup of Chicken Stock, bring to a boil.

Simmer for 20 minutes. Drain.

Mix all ingredients together and keep warm until ready to serve.

This is great for Thanksgiving or Christmas dinner.

Makes 4 cups

Coconut-Curry Basmati Rice

4	cups **basmati rice**, cooked
1½	teaspoons **curry powder**
1	cup unsweetened **coconut milk**
3	tablespoons **cilantro**, chopped

Mix all ingredients in a bowl.

Serve warm.

This is great with an Asian grilled fish.

Makes 4 cups

Orzo, Wild Mushroom *and* Serrano Ham

½ cup **Serrano ham**, diced
1 cup **leeks**, thinly sliced
½ cup **shitake mushrooms**, sliced
½ cup **button mushrooms**, sliced
½ cup **portobello mushrooms**, sliced
½ cup **oyster mushrooms**, sliced
½ teaspoon **kosher salt**
1 tablespoon **lemon zest**
1 tablespoon fresh **thyme**, finely chopped
¼ teaspoon **black pepper**
¼ cup **Chicken Stock** (see page 16)
2 cups **orzo pasta**, cooked
¼ cup assorted **Greek olives**, pitted and chopped*
¼ cup **olive oil**

Place olive oil in saucepan and heat.

Add Serrano ham and lightly cook.

Add leeks and cook until soft. Remove with slotted spoon.

Add mushrooms and cook until brown.

Add salt, zest, thyme, pepper and cooked leek mixture.

Add Chicken Stock and bring to a boil. Reduce to low and cook until liquid is absorbed.

Add to cooked orzo pasta and mix well.

Add Greek olives and toss together. Keep warm until ready to use.

You can find these and other types of olives in the deli section of most markets.

This is great on grilled lamb chops.

Makes 4 cups

Garlic Olive Mashers

3 lbs. **Idaho potatoes**, peeled
¼ cup **Olive Oil Vegetable Garlic Sauce** (see page 189)
2 **garlic** cloves, roasted
3 tablespoons **butter**, melted
½ teaspoon **Lawrys Seasoning Salt**
½ teaspoon **white pepper**
½ cup **Half & Half**
¼ cup **sour cream**
½ cup assorted **Greek olives**, pitted*

Cook potatoes in boiling water until soft, about 30 minutes.

Drain and place in mixer.

Purée roasted garlic with Olive Oil Garlic Sauce.

Add with remaining ingredients to cooked potatoes and mix until well blended.

Keep warm until ready to serve.

You can find these and other types of olives in the deli section of most markets.

These are one of my favorite side dishes, they go well with anything!

Makes 6 cups

Goat Cheese Potato Cake

2   cups **Potato Leek Cake Mix** (see page 149)
½   cup **goat cheese**, softened

Place ingredients in mixing bowl and mix well.

Form into ¼ cup round patties, place on griddle and cook until golden.

Serve warm.

These are great with grilled meats.

Makes 4 cakes

Fingerling Potatoes

2½   lbs. **fingerling potatoes**, bias cut
¼   cup **olive oil**
¼   cup **butter**, melted
1   small **leek**, diced

Cook fingerling potatoes in boiling water until soft. Drain.

Put olive oil and butter in large sauté pan and heat.

Add leeks and cook until translucent.

Add fingerlings and sauté until golden brown.

These go well with fish, pork and chicken. We use these potatoes for the Olive Oil Poached Halibut in the Seafood Chapter.

Makes 4 cups

Wasabi Mashers

3   lbs. **Idaho potatoes**, peeled
3   tablespoons **Olive Oil Vegetable Garlic Sauce**
       (see page 189)
1   tablespoon **butter**, melted
1   tablespoon **Wasabi Butter**, melted (see page 113)
1   tablespoon **Wasabi Paste** (see recipe on right)
2   teaspoons **Lawry's Seasoning Salt**
½   teaspoon **white pepper**
½   cup **Half & Half**
¼   cup **sour cream**

Cook potatoes in boiling water until soft, about 30 minutes.

Drain and place in mixer.

Add remaining ingredients and mix until well blended.

Keep warm until ready to use.

Makes 6 cups

Wasabi Paste

¼   cup **wasabi powder**
2   tablespoons **water**

Mix together thoroughly and refrigerate until ready to use.

Use these as a side dish when preparing anything Asian, especially sea bass or ahi tuna.

Creole Chicken Breast Stuffing

1	lb. **Andouille sausage**, chopped
5	tablespoons **jalapeño pepper**, roasted, finely chopped
1	cup **red onion**, finely chopped
10	**garlic** cloves, roasted, finely chopped
1	cup **mushrooms**, chopped, ¼" dice
3	cups **Jalapeño Cornbread Crumbs** (see page 61)
1	tablespoon fresh **rosemary**, finely chopped
1	tablespoon fresh **thyme**, finely chopped
1	tablespoon fresh **sage**, finely chopped
½	cup **cider vinegar**
½	cup **apple cider**
1	tablespoon fresh **parsley**, finely chopped
½	cup **olive oil**
1	teaspoon **salt**
½	teaspoon **black pepper**

Sauté Andouille sausage on medium heat until it starts to brown in large saucepan.

Add jalapeño peppers, onions and garlic. Cook until tender, about 3–4 minutes.

Add mushrooms and cook 3–5 minutes. Cool.

When cool, fold in Jalapeño Cornbread Crumbs, spices, vinegar, cider, parsley, olive oil, salt and pepper.

This is a great use for extra Jalapeño Cornbread from the Steak Salad recipe. Use this in Pork Loin also.

Makes 4 cups

Sautéed Spinach

½	cup **olive oil**
2	**garlic** cloves, finely chopped
4	cups **spinach**, stems removed
12	**red grape tomatoes**
4	teaspoons **Parmesan cheese**
1	**lemon**, cut in half

Add olive oil to sauté pan and heat. Add garlic and cook until golden.

Add spinach and toss well.

Add tomatoes and Parmesan cheese and mix well.

Squeeze lemon into spinach and serve immediately.

We use this recipe on the Parmesan Crusted Whitefish.

Serves 4

Rice Pilaf

1	cup	**butter**
1	cup	**red onions**, finely chopped
1½	lbs.	**Uncle Ben's Rice**
1	teaspoon	**kosher salt**
2	cups	**Vegetable Stock** (see page 19)
2	cups	**Chicken Stock** (see page 16)

Preheat oven to 350°.

Melt butter until hot in saucepan.

Add onions and cook until soft.

Add raw rice and salt. Toss the rice for 2–3 minutes.

Pour the stocks on the rice and mix well.

Bring rice to a boil.

Remove from stove and place in oven. Cook for 20 minutes.

Remove from oven. Mix well. Ready to serve.

Serves 6

Spinach, Figs, Chanterelles *and* Prosciutto

½	cup	**olive oil**
½	cup	**proscuitto ham**, finely julienned
½	cup	**chanterelle mushrooms**, sliced
4	cups	**spinach**
8		dried **black mission figs**, sliced
		sea salt

Heat oil in sauté pan.

Add proscuitto and chanterelles and cook lightly.

Add spinach and figs. Toss well, add sea salt and cook until soft.

This is great with grilled lamb chops and the Olive Oil Poached Halibut in the Seafood Chapter.

Serves 4

Honey Glazed Carrots

1	lb. **baby carrots,** peeled, blanched, stem on
¼	cup **honey**
2	tablespoons **butter**
2	tablespoons **brown sugar**

Preheat oven to 350°.

Place carrots in saucepan and cover with water. Bring to a boil and drain.

Toss carrots with honey, butter and brown sugar and place in baking pan.

Place in oven and roast until carrots are cooked and golden, about 30 minutes.

Ready to serve.

Serves 4

Whipped Sweet Potatoes

3½	lbs. **sweet potatoes,** peeled, cut into 2"cubes
1	**Granny Smith apple,** small, peeled, cored, grated
¼	cup **whipping cream**
2	tablespoons **butter**
2	teaspoons **brown sugar**
1	teaspoon **maple syrup**
1½	teaspoons **kosher salt**
¼	teaspoon **black pepper**

Put sweet potatoes and grated apple into saucepot. Cover with water and cook until tender, about 30 minutes.

Drain, and transfer to mixer and mash. Gradually add all ingredients and mix well until fluffy.

Serves 6

Yukon Gold Potato Gratin

3	tablespoons **Gorgonzola cheese**, crumbled
½	cup **heavy cream**
¼	teaspoon **kosher salt**
⅛	teaspoon **black pepper**
2	teaspoons **butter**
1	**garlic** clove, finely chopped
2	teaspoons **shallots**, finely chopped
¼	teaspoon fresh **thyme**, chopped
¼	teaspoon fresh **rosemary**, chopped
1	lb. **Yukon gold potatoes**, sliced very thin

Mix cheese, ¼ cup cream, salt and pepper in medium mixing bowl. Form into paste.

Add remaining cream. Mix well.

In sauté pan melt butter. Add garlic and shallots and cook until soft.

Add thyme and rosemary. Add butter mixture to cream mix. Mix well.

In a small baking dish layer potatoes and cream mixture from the bottom up in the following way:

⅓	cup cream mixture
½	cup potatoes
⅓	cup cream mixture
½	cup potatoes
⅓	cup cream mixture
½	cup potatoes
⅓	cup cream mixture

Cover with foil and bake at 350° for 45 minutes. Uncover and bake for 20 minutes more.

Serves 6

Potato Leek Cake Mix

1	lb. **Yukon Gold potatoes**, peeled
¼	teaspoon **salt**
	pinch **black pepper**
1	**egg**, lightly beaten
¼	cup **leeks**, finely chopped, sautéed in butter
2	tablespoons **butter**

Bring water to a boil in a large stockpot. Add potatoes and boil for 15 minutes. Remove from heat and allow to rest for 10 minutes.

Drain potatoes under slowly running cool water for 10 minutes. Refrigerate for 30 minutes.

Peel cooled potatoes and shred into large bowl. Season with salt and pepper. Add beaten egg and leeks, stir gently. Shape into 4 patties.

Heat butter in skillet and sauté patties over medium heat until golden, approximately 3 to 4 minutes.

Makes 4 cakes

White Cheddar Mashers

3	lbs. **Idaho potatoes**, peeled
¼	cup **Olive Oil Garlic & Herb Sauce** (see page 14)
¼	lb. **white cheddar cheese**
2	tablespoons **butter**, melted
2	teaspoons **seasoning salt**
½	teaspoon **white pepper**
½	cup **Half & Half**
¼	cup **sour cream**

Cook potatoes in boiling water until soft, approximately 30 minutes.

Drain and transfer to large mixing bowl and slowly mash potatoes. Add remaining ingredients and beat until well blended.

Makes 4 cups

Lobster Mashers

3	lbs. **Idaho potatoes**, peeled
3	tablespoons **Olive Oil Vegetable Garlic Sauce** (see page 189)
1	tablespoon **butter**, melted
1	cup **lobster meat**, chopped into 1" pieces
2	teaspoons **Lawry's Seasoning Salt**
½	teaspoon **white pepper**
½	cup **Half & Half**
¼	cup **sour cream**

Cook potatoes in boiling water until soft, about 30 minutes.

Drain and place in mixer.

Add remaining ingredients and mix until well blended.

Keep warm until ready to use.

This is a great side dish with the salmon in the Seafood Chapter.

Makes 6 cups

Basil Mashers

3	lbs. **Idaho potatoes**
¼	cup **Olive Oil Vegetable Garlic Sauce** (see page 189)
2	tablespoons **butter**, melted
2	teaspoons **Lawry's Seasoning Salt**
1	teaspoon **white pepper**
½	cup **Half & Half**
¼	cup **sour cream**
3	tablespoons **Basil Pesto** (see page 45)

Cook potatoes in boiling water until soft, about 30 minutes.

Drain and place in mixer.

Add remaining ingredients and mix until well blended.

Keep warm until ready to serve.

Makes 6 cups

Everyone looks forward to dessert and so do I. This chapter is always a fun one to write. Desserts are usually the crowning touch to a wonderful meal. Try any one of these recipes and the rewards will be waiting for you and your lucky guests.

Dessert

Fresh Berries Grand Marnier

1 cup fresh **blackberries**,
whole, cleaned

1 cup fresh **strawberries**,
whole, cleaned

1 cup fresh **raspberries**, cleaned

1 cup fresh **blueberries**, cleaned

4 fresh sprigs **mint leaves**

1 cup **Crème Fraîche Mixture**
(see recipe below)

Crème Fraîche Mixture

¼ cup **whipping cream**

½ cup **Crème Fraîche**

2 tablespoons **Grand Marnier**

¼ cup **brown sugar**

Place the whipping cream into mixing bowl and whip until stiff.

Add the other ingredients blending slowly into the whipped cream by folding gently with a rubber spatula.

Evenly distribute the fresh berries in alternating pattern around outside of plate (or use a parfait glass and layer berries evenly in glasses).

Place ¼ cup of the Crème Fraîche Mixture in the center (or on top of berries) and add the fresh sprig of mint.

Berry Napoleon *with* Lemon Curd

Lemon Curd

6		**egg yolks**
2		**eggs**
½	cup	**sugar**
¼	cup fresh	**lemon juice**
1	teaspoon fresh	**lime zest**
1	teaspoon	**orange zest**
1	teaspoon	**lemon zest**
¼	cup	**butter**, melted
12	pieces	**puff pastry sheet**, 2" x 5" x ⅛"

Fresh Berries

2	cups mixed fresh berries, (**strawberries, blackberries, raspberries**)
2	tablespoons **Grand Marnier**
2	teaspoons **super fine sugar**

Raspberry Sauce

2	pints **raspberries**, (thawed if using frozen)
¼	cup **raspberry preserves**
1	tablespoon fresh **lemon juice**
1	tablespoon fresh **mint**, finely julienned

Egg Wash

1	**egg**, lightly beaten
2	tablespoons **heavy cream**

For Lemon Curd Beat the egg yolks and the eggs with the sugar until extremely thick in mixing bowl.

Place mixing bowl in double boiler over medium heat. Gradually add the lemon juice and whisk well until the curd thickens heavily.

Add the zests and gradually add the melted butter. Remove from double boiler and cool completely.

For Puff Pastry Roll out puff pastry ⅛" thick. Cut into 2" x 5" rectangle pieces.

Brush with Egg Wash.

Bake at 350° until golden. Cool.

For Napoleon Place 1 tablespoon of Lemon Curd on top of one puff pastry piece.

Place one cup of fresh berries on top of lemon curd.

Place another pastry rectangle on top of berries.

Place 1 tablespoon of Lemon Curd on top of puff pastry piece.

Place some berries on top of pastry.

Drizzle Raspberry Sauce around napoleon.

Dust with powdered sugar.

For Raspberry Sauce Place raspberries and raspberry preserves in the bowl of a food processor with the metal blade and purée. Strain into a bowl. Add lemon juice and mint; mix well.

For Egg Wash Mix together well.

Coconut Pecan Tart

1	cup **coconut**, toasted
⅔	cup **pecan halves**, chopped, toasted
½	cup **butter**, melted
⅓	cup **brown sugar**
1	teaspoon **almond extract**
¼	cup **sweetened coconut milk**
6	**egg yolks**
⅛	teaspoon **salt**
1	**Chocolate Wafer Crust** (see recipe below)

Chocolate Wafer Crust
(Makes 1 tart)

1	package **chocolate wafers** (9 oz. package)
½	cup **butter**, melted

Presentation

1	**Coconut Pecan Tart**
1	oz. **Bittersweet Chocolate Sauce** (see page 176)
1	scoop **coffee ice cream** **powdered sugar**, for dusting

Preheat oven to 275°.

Toast coconut and pecans in oven for 5 minutes at 275° until golden.

Mix butter, brown sugar, almond extract and coconut milk in bowl and mix well.

Add egg yolks and salt and mix well.

Add coconut and nuts and mix well.

Pour filling into 9-inch springform pan over Chocolate Wafer Crust and place in oven for 30–35 minutes or until golden.

Allow to cool.

Cut each tart into 10 pieces.

For Chocolate Wafer Crust In food processor finely grate chocolate wafers.

Add melted butter.

Place crumbs in a 9-inch springform pan.

Press crumbs to cover bottom of pan and halfway up sides of pan.

For Presentation Place tart on serving plate.

Drizzle Bittersweet Chocolate Sauce over tart.

Place scoop of ice cream next to tart.

Dust with powdered sugar.

Espresso Panna Cotta

2 tablespoons **gelatin**

2 cups **milk**

4 cups **heavy cream**

1 teaspoon **vanilla extract**

2 teaspoons **ground espresso beans**

1⅓ cups **semisweet chocolate**, chopped

4 tablespoons **bittersweet chocolate**, chopped

2 tablespoons **sugar**

8 tablespoons **whipped cream**

16 fresh **raspberries**, 2 for each portion

8 tablespoons **Bittersweet Chocolate Sauce** (see page 176)

powdered sugar, for dusting

Place gelatin in the milk until softened.

Bring cream, vanilla extract, espresso beans, chocolates and sugar to barely a simmer. Add the milk and gelatin and stir to dissolve gelatin.

Strain and pour mixture evenly into eight, 10 oz. wine glasses.

Place in refrigerator for 4 hours to set.

Top with whipped cream and two raspberries.

Drizzle with Bittersweet Chocolate Sauce and dust with powdered sugar.

Ice Cream Toppings

Peanut Brittle
(Makes 2 cups)

½	cup	**water**
2	cups	**sugar**
¼	teaspoon	**cream of tartar**
1	cup	**light corn syrup**
2	tablespoons	**butter**
2	cups	**roasted peanuts**
1	teaspoon	**baking soda**

Butterscotch Sauce
(Makes 2 cups)

¼	cup	**butter**
½	cup	**dark brown sugar**
1	tablespoon	**water**
⅓	cup	**light corn syrup**
⅓	cup	**whipping cream**

Hot Fudge Sauce
(Makes 2 cups)

⅔	cup	**heavy cream**
½	cup	**corn syrup**
⅓	cup	**dark brown sugar**
¼	cup	**cocoa powder**
¼	teaspoon	**salt**
6	oz.	**bittersweet chocolate**
2	tablespoons	**butter**
1	teaspoon	**vanilla**

Combine water, sugar, cream of tartar and corn syrup in saucepan.

Bring to a boil over medium heat until golden.

Stir in butter until melted.

Stir in the peanuts.

Stir in the baking soda.

Pour mixture onto lined sheet tray. Allow to cool.

Chop and store in an airtight container.

For Butterscotch Sauce Melt butter.

Stir in both sugars, water and corn syrup. Bring to a boil.

Boil for 2 minutes. Cool for 15 minutes.

Whisk in cream.

Keep at room temperature.

This is fantastic over ice cream with our homemade peanut brittle.

For Hot Fudge Sauce Bring cream, corn syrup, sugar, cocoa, salt and ½ of the chocolate to a boil over medium heat until chocolate has melted.

Reduce heat to low and cook for 3–4 minutes.

Add butter, vanilla and remaining chocolate and stir until smooth. Cool.

The Grill's Chocolate Attack

8   3" round pieces **Chocolate Buttermilk Cake,** (plus trimming for top) (see recipe below)

2   pints fresh **raspberries**

4   tablespoons **Crème de Cassis**

4   cups **Chocolate Praline Mousse** (see opposite page)

8   tablespoons **White Chocolate Curls** (from ½ lb. white chocolate bar)

8   tablespoons **Dark Chocolate Curls** (from ½ lb. dark chocolate bar)

1   cup **Cinnamon Crème Anglaise** (see opposite page)

¼   cup **Raspberry Sauce** (see page 155)

1   cup **Mocha Crème Anglaise** (see opposite page)

    powdered sugar, for dusting

Chocolate Buttermilk Cake
(Makes 8 Chocolate Attacks)

1½   cups **all-purpose flour**

1   cup **cocoa powder**

2   teaspoons **baking powder**

2   teaspoons **baking soda**

⅛   teaspoon **salt**

2¼   cups **sugar**

1   cup **buttermilk**

5   **eggs,** room temperature

2   teaspoons **vanilla extract**

⅓   cup **butter,** melted

1   cup **coffee,** room temperature

Cut cake into 3" circles with a pastry ring.

Place raspberries on top of cake circles. Sprinkle with Crème de Cassis.

Using a pastry bag with a star tip, pipe Chocolate Praline Mousse on top of berries covering berries evenly.

Top with chocolate cake trimmings so that the mouse is covered well.

Top with White and Dark Chocolate Curls.

The recipe can be set up ahead of time up to this step.

Place finished cake onto serving plate.

Drizzle 2 tablespoons Cinnamon Crème Anglaise around cake.

Zig zag 2 teaspoons Raspberry Sauce and 2 tablespoons Mocha Crème Anglaise over top of dessert.

Dust with powdered sugar.

For Chocolate Curls Allow chocolate bars to get to room temperature.

With a sharp peeler, shave down the sides of the chocolate bars.

Cinnamon Crème Anglaise
(Makes 1½ cups)

1¼	cups	**heavy cream**
⅛	teaspoon	**cinnamon**
½	teaspoon	**vanilla extract**
4		**egg yolks**
⅓	cup	**sugar**

Mocha Crème Anglaise *(Makes 2 cups)*

4		**egg yolks**
½	cup	**sugar**
½	teaspoon	**ground espresso**
1	cup	**heavy cream**
1	cup	**Half and Half**
⅓	cup	**chocolate**, finely chopped
½	teaspoon	**vanilla extract**

Chocolate Praline Mousse
(Makes 4 cups)

Almond Praline

1½	cups	**almonds**, sliced
1½	cups	**sugar**
½	cup	**water**
1	teaspoon	fresh **lemon juice**

Chocolate Mousse

2	cups	**semi-sweet chocolate**, pulverized
4	teaspoons	**gelatin**
1	cup	**milk**
1	cup	**Almond Praline** (see recipe above)
2	tablespoons	**vegetable oil**
2	tablespoons	**vanilla extract**
2	cups	**whipping cream**

For Chocolate Buttermilk Cake Preheat oven to 300°.

Sift together flour, cocoa powder, baking powder, baking soda, salt and sugar in a mixing bowl.

In another mixing bowl whisk the buttermilk, eggs and vanilla until well combined.

In a saucepan, melt butter and stir in coffee. Whisk into buttermilk mixture and then combine with dry ingredients.

Pour mixture into 9 x 12-inch pan that has been sprayed with Pam.

Bake for 40 minutes. Allow to cool.

Cut cake with 3" stainless steel pastry rings and leave trimmings for the rest of the dessert topping.

For Cinnamon Crème Anglaise Bring cream, cinnamon and vanilla to a boil in a saucepan, stirring constantly.

In a mixing bowl whisk egg yolks and sugar until pale in color.

Pour ¼ of the hot cream into yolk mixture and mix very well.

Pour the yolk mixture into the remaining hot cream and cook over medium heat until thickens and coats back of spoon.

Strain and stir until cool.

For Mocha Crème Anglaise Whisk egg yolks in stainless steel bowl with the sugar and espresso.

In a saucepan bring cream and Half and Half to a gentle boil over medium heat.

Remove and whisk into egg yolk mixture.

Remove and strain. Add chopped chocolate. Let stand 30 seconds then whisk until smooth.

Chill. Stir in vanilla.

For Praline Toast almonds in 350° oven for 10 minutes or until golden in color.

Lightly butter a cookie sheet.

Combine sugar, water and lemon juice in saucepan and cook over medium heat until sugar dissolves. Raise the heat to medium high and bring syrup to a boil. Boil for 5 to 10 minutes until syrup caramelizes and turns to dark amber in color.

Remove pan from heat and add almonds. Pour onto buttered cookie sheet. Cool.

Place in food processor and pulverize.

For Mousse Process chocolate in food processor until finely chopped. Add gelatin to chocolate.*

In saucepan bring milk to a boil over medium heat.

With the motor running, pour milk into chocolate and process for 15 seconds until chocolate has melted.

Add the Almond Praline, oil and vanilla. Process for 15 seconds until mixture is smooth and creamy. Scrape into mixing bowl and cool.

In a separate bowl, whip the cream until soft peaks form.

Gently fold ⅓ of the cream into the chocolate mixture. Fold in the remaining cream. Do not overfold.

Allow to cool before using in Chocolate Attack dessert.

*Adding gelatin in chocolate first, gives better consistency in finished chocolate. Adding hot milk will allow it to dissolve.

This recipe takes time and good organization, but you will wow your guests every time.

Chocolate Malted Milk Pudding

1 quart **milk**
4 tablespoons **cornstarch**
1 cup **malted milk powder**
4 tablespoons **cocoa powder**
pinch **salt**
¼ cup **semi-sweet chocolate chips**
6 tablespoons **sugar**
1 teaspoon **vanilla extract**

Individual Pudding

½ cup **Chocolate Malted Milk Pudding**
(see recipe above)
¼ cup **Chocolate Brownie Pieces**
(see opposite page)
1 tablespoon **White Chocolate Cream**
(see recipe below)
1 tablespoon **White Chocolate Curls**
(from white chocolate bar)
powdered sugar, for dusting

White Chocolate Cream
(Makes 1 cup)

⅓ cup **white chocolate**, chopped
2 tablespoons **milk**
½ cup **whipped cream**, stiff
¼ teaspoon **vanilla extract**

For Pudding Blend 1 cup milk with cornstarch.

In saucepan, combine malted milk powder, cocoa powder and salt.

Slowly whisk in remaining milk, chocolate chips and sugar. Cook over medium heat stirring until chocolate is melted.

Whisk in milk/cornstarch mixture and cook over low heat until very thick, almost to a boil, about 10 minutes.

Remove from stove and stir in vanilla. Refrigerate until well chilled.

For White Chocolate Cream Melt white chocolate in double boiler over warm simmering water until smooth. Remove from heat.

Bring milk to a simmer in saucepan and whisk into melted white chocolate. Allow to cool.

Add to whipped cream and vanilla, mix well. Keep refrigerated until ready to use.

For Chocolate Brownies Preheat oven to 325°.

Sift together flour, cocoa and baking powder. Set aside.

Melt butter and semisweet chocolate pieces in a double boiler. Set aside.

Place eggs, sugar and vanilla in a mixing bowl and beat until thick. Stir in chocolate mixture. Add dry ingredients and stir until just blended. Do not over mix. Stir in sour cream.

Pour into a greased 10 x 12-inch baking pan. Bake in oven for 1 hour. Remove from oven and allow to cool before serving.

Chocolate Brownies *(Makes 12 pieces)*

½   cup **all-purpose flour**
4   tablespoons **cocoa powder**
1   tablespoon **baking powder**
½   cup **butter**
1¼ cups **semisweet chocolate** pieces
6   **eggs**
2   cups **sugar**
2   teaspoons **vanilla extract**
½   cup **sour cream**

For Presentation Place 2 tablespoons of pudding in bottom of double espresso coffee cup, or other serving dish. Top with ¼ cup crumbled brownie pieces.

Add ⅓ cup of Chocolate Malted Milk Pudding on top of Chocolate Brownies.

Top with 1 tablespoon of White Chocolate Cream and sprinkle with a few more brownie pieces.

Add White Chocolate Curls on top and dust with powdered sugar.

Chocolate Fallen Cake

6   pieces **Chocolate Cake**
        (see recipe below)
6   tablespoons **semi-sweet
        chocolate chips**
6   scoops **caramel toffee ice cream**
6   tablespoons **Toffee Pecans**
        (see recipe below)
6   tablespoons **powdered sugar**,
        for dusting
6   tablespoons **Carmel Sauce**
        (see recipe below)

Chocolate Cake

12   oz. **bittersweet chocolate**
1   cup **butter**
1   cup **sugar**
½   cup **all-purpose flour**
6   **eggs**

Toffee Pecans

¼   cup **butter**
⅓   cup **sugar**
1   teaspoon **salt**
1   cup **pecan halves**

Caramel Sauce

1   cup **sugar**
¼   cup **water**
½   cup **whipping cream**
2   teaspoons **vanilla extract**

For Presentation Warm chocolate cake in 250° oven for 8 minutes or use microwave at 45 seconds at high level.

Remove cake from ramekin and place in center of serving plate. Place scoop of caramel ice cream next to cake.

Sprinkle with Toffee Pecans around Chocolate Cake and ice cream.

Drizzle Caramel Sauce over top of Chocolate Cake and ice cream. Dust with powdered sugar.

For Chocolate Cake Preheat oven to 350°.

Spray six, 8 oz. tall china ramekins with vegetable spray.

Place chocolate and butter in the top of double boiler over medium heat and melt. Cool slightly.

Place sugar, flour and eggs in large bowl and beat until thick and fluffy. Gently beat in chocolate mixture.

Pour batter in ramekins, filling them almost to the top of the ramekin. Bake for 20 minutes.

Remove from oven and place 1 tablespoon of chocolate chips into top of each warm cake.

Allow to cool.

For Toffee Pecans Place butter in a small saucepan over medium heat. Cook until melted.

Add sugar and salt and mix well. Add pecans and mix well. Cook until sugar caramelizes and coats nuts, about 5 minutes.

When sugar is turning dark brown, pour onto cookie sheet. Spread pecans apart with fork and allow to cool.

For Caramel Sauce Combine sugar and water in stainless steel saucepan. Dissolve sugar over low heat.

Increase heat and cook until the caramel is a golden amber color.

Remove from stove and slowly add the whipping cream, 2 tablespoons at a time, stirring with a wooden spoon. Add vanilla and mix well.

Lemon Almond Pound Cake *with* Fresh Berries *and* Lemon Cream

SERVES 8

8 pieces **Lemon Almond Pound Cake**,
    cut in half
8 scoops **vanilla bean ice cream**
2 cups **Fresh Berry Mix**
8 tablespoons **Lemon Cream**
    (see recipe below)
powdered sugar, for dusting

Fresh Berry Mix
1 cup **strawberries**
½ cup **raspberries**
½ cup **blackberries**
1 tablespoon fresh **mint**
1 teaspoon **sugar**

Lemon Cream
16 oz. **Lemon Curd** (see page 155)
8 oz. **whipped cream**

Place ½ piece of pound cake on each serving plate.

Place scoop of ice cream on top of cake.

Place other half of pound cake angled on ice cream.

Place ½ cup Fresh Berry Mix around Lemon Almond Pound Cake. Top with Lemon Cream and dust with powdered sugar.

For Lemon Cream Whip cream until stiff. Add Lemon Curd and mix well. Refrigerate until ready to use.

For Fresh Berry Mix Mix all ingredients together and keep cold until ready to use.

Return to the Common Grill

Lemon Almond Pound Cake

1   cup **sliced almonds**, toasted
1   cup **sugar**
1   cup **butter**, softened
4   **eggs**
1   tablespoon **lemon zest**
1   cup **all-purpose flour**
1   teaspoon **baking powder**
¼   teaspoon **salt**
¼   cup fresh **lemon juice**

Preheat oven to 300°.

Grind almonds and sugar in food processor until finely chopped.

Cream the butter, add sugar and almonds until light and fluffy.

Add eggs, one at a time and mix in lemon zest.

Sift flour, baking powder and salt in separate bowl.

Beat the dry ingredients and lemon juice into the butter mixture half at a time. Mix thoroughly after each addition.

Pour batter into 9" springform pan and bake for 45–60 minutes.

Cool and cut into 8 pieces.

Sweet *and* Sour Cherry Cobbler

3	cups	**bing cherries**, pitted
3	cups	**tart cherries**, pitted
½	cup	**sugar**
	pinch	**kosher salt**
¼	teaspoon	**vanilla extract**
1½	tablespoons	**butter**, melted
¼	teaspoon	**cinnamon**
2	tablespoons	**tapioca flour**

Topping

⅓	cup	**butter**, softened
½	cup	**brown sugar**
1	cup	**sugar**
1	teaspoon	**cinnamon**
1½	cups	**all-purpose flour**

Preheat oven to 300°.

Mix all ingredients together.

Place 1 cup filling in six, 8 oz. ceramic ramekins and top with ¼ cup cobbler topping.

Place in oven for 30 minutes or until golden.

Place scoop of vanilla bean ice cream on top of cobbler and serve.

For Topping Place soft butter into mixing bowl, add brown sugar, sugar, cinnamon and mix well.

Add flour and mix well until all ingredients are mixed thoroughly.

Peach Brown Betty

3	cups **Challah (egg bread) bread crumbs**, soft
1	cup **brown sugar**
¼	cup **sugar**
1	teaspoon **allspice**
1	teaspoon **cinnamon**
5	lbs. **peach slices**, peeled, quartered, sliced into ½" pieces
2	teaspoons fresh **lemon juice**
⅓	cup cold **butter**, cut in pieces

Preheat oven to 350°.

Spray eight, 8 oz. glass bowls with vegetable spray.

In a small bowl, toss the bread crumbs with brown sugar, sugar, allspice and cinnamon, mix well.

In a medium bowl toss the peaches with the lemon juice.

Scatter 2 tablespoons of the crumb mixture in the bottom of each glass bowl, cover with half of the peaches.

Drizzle 2 tablespoons of water on top, add less than half of the crumb mixture over the peaches.

Dot with half of the cold butter on top.

Top with the remaining peaches.

Add the rest of the cold butter and top with the remaining crumb mixture.

Place in pre-heated oven and bake for 45 minutes or until crumbs are nicely browned.

Serve warm with vanilla ice cream.

Lemon Cheesecake *with* Blueberry Sauce *and* Lemon Sabayon

MAKES ONE 9" CAKE

Ginger Snap Crust

¾	cup **ginger snap cookies**, finely ground
¾	cup **graham cracker crumbs**, finely ground
3	tablespoons **macadamia nuts**, toasted, finely ground
3	tablespoons **butter**, melted

Cheesecake Filling

2	lbs. **cream cheese**, softened
1	cup **mascarpone cheese**, softened
½	cup **sugar**
2	**eggs**
2	teaspoons **lemon zest**, finely chopped
2	tablespoons fresh **lemon juice**

Cheesecake

Blueberry Sauce (see recipe below)
Lemon Sabayon (see recipe below)

Blueberry Sauce *(Makes 4 cups)*

4	cups **blueberries**, fresh, washed
⅔	cup **sugar**
2	tablespoons **water**
1	tablespoon fresh **lemon juice**

Lemon Sabayon Sauce *(Makes 2 cups)*

8	**egg yolks**
½	cup **sugar**
¼	teaspoon **salt**
¼	cup **rum**
½	cup fresh **lemon juice**

For Ginger Snap Crust Preheat oven to 300°.

Combine ingredients in mixing bowl and mix well.

Press crumbs into 9-inch springform pan and bake in oven for 5 minutes. Allow to cool.

Note: Make sure crust is 2" high on sides.

For Cheesecake Preheat oven to 300°.

Combine cream cheese, mascarpone cheese and sugar in mixer using paddle attachment. Mix until smooth.

Mix in eggs, zest and lemon juice. Mix well.

Pour into pre-baked crust.

Cook in water bath in preheated oven for about one hour or until set. Allow to cool.

Cut into 10 pieces. Place on serving plate.

Top with 3 tablespoons of Blueberry Sauce and 2 tablespoons Lemon Sabayon.

For Blueberry Sauce Mix all ingredients together in a saucepan. Cook over low heat for 5 minutes until thick.

Purée ½ and then add back.

Mix well and refrigerate.

For Lemon Sabayon Sauce Combine egg yolks, sugar and salt in mixing bowl.

Whisk in rum and lemon juice.

Place bowl over double boiler on medium heat and whisk for 3–4 minutes until thick and tripled.

Immediately cool down over bowl with ice and whisk until cold.

Return to the Common Grill

White Chocolate-Banana Crème Brulée

2 cups **whipping cream**

¼ cup **sugar**

½ cup **white chocolate**, chopped

1 teaspoon **vanilla extract**

5 **egg yolks**

1 teaspoon **superfine sugar**

3 **bananas**, sliced

Heat cream, sugar and white chocolate to a low simmer. Turn off heat.

Add egg yolks to cream and whisk well.

Add vanilla to mixture and blend.

Pour custard evenly into six, 6 oz. crème brulée dishes and place in water bath.

Place in oven at 250° and cook for 45–60 minutes until light brown on top.

Cool and cover not letting plastic wrap touch custard.

Add 4 slices banana to top of each custard. Sprinkle with sugar evenly over top of banana and custard. Using butane torch caramelize sugar until slightly burnt.

Malted Milk Chocolate Crème Brulée

5   **egg yolks**
1   cup **milk**
2   cups **whipping cream**
⅛   teaspoon **salt**
⅔   cup **sugar**
1   tablespoon **malted milk powder**
⅓   cup **semi-sweet chocolate,**
        finely chopped
5   **eggs**
1   teaspoon **superfine sugar**
     Bittersweet Chocolate Sauce
        (see page 176)

Bring milk, whipping cream, salt, sugar and malted milk powder to a gentle boil.

Add chocolate, let it melt about 60 seconds, then add eggs.

Pour evenly into six, 6 oz. crème brulée dishes. In a water bath, bake at 325° for 60 minutes.

Remove from oven and allow to cool and set.

Sprinkle each brulée with superfine sugar and caramelize with a blow torch until golden.

Drizzle Bittersweet Chocolate Sauce over top of brulée.

Peanut Butter Cheesecake

1½   cups **graham cracker crumbs**
½   cup **honey roasted peanuts**
½   cup **butter**, melted
2   lbs. **cream cheese**
1   cup **sugar**
4   **eggs**
2   teaspoons **vanilla extract**
1   cup **peanut butter**, creamy

Cheesecake

1   piece **Peanut Butter Cheesecake**
2   tablespoons **Bittersweet Chocolate Sauce** (see recipe below)
2   tablespoons **Peanut Brittle**, broken up (see page 159)

Bittersweet Chocolate Sauce

1   cup **cocoa powder**
½   cup **sugar**
1½   cups **water**
½   cup **cream**
4   tablespoons **bittersweet chocolate**
2   tablespoons **butter**

For Crust Place graham cracker crumbs and honey roasted peanuts in food processor and finely chop.

Add melted butter and combine well.

Bring crust halfway up side of 9-inch springform pan and cover bottom.

For Cake Preheat oven to 300°.

Beat cream cheese in mixer until smooth.

Slowly add sugar and beat until there are no lumps.

Add eggs one at a time, then the vanilla.

Add peanut butter; mix until combined.

Pour into prepared springform pan.

Bake in water bath in preheated oven for 55 to 60 minutes or until set. Allow to cool.

Cut into 10 pieces.

For Cheesecake Place Peanut Butter Cheesecake on serving plate.

Sprinkle Peanut Brittle on top and around cheesecake. Drizzle with Bittersweet Chocolate Sauce.

For Bittersweet Chocolate Sauce Combine cocoa, sugar, and water in a saucepan. Bring to a boil and cook for 5 minutes, while whisking constantly.

Stir in the cream: return to a boil and continue cooking for 2 to 3 minutes.

Remove from heat and whisk in chocolate and butter. Return to heat and bring to a boil.

Immediately remove from heat once chocolate boils. Serve warm.

Peach-Plum-Nectarine Cornmeal Crisp

4   cups **peaches**, fresh thinly sliced
2   cups **plums**, fresh thinly sliced
2   cups **nectarines**, fresh thinly sliced
2   tablespoons **flour**
2½   tablespoons **sugar**
1   teaspoon fresh **lemon juice**
      pinch **salt**

Cornmeal Topping
½   cup **brown sugar**
1   teaspoon **cinnamon**
½   cup **flour**
½   cup **yellow cornmeal**
1   lb. **butter**, softened

For Cornmeal Topping Combine all ingredients together in mixer and blend well.

For Crisp Preheat oven to 350°.

Combine all ingredients together in a mixing bowl and mix well.

Place evenly in six, 8 oz. ramekins and fill full to the top.

Top with Cornmeal Topping.

Place in oven and bake for 30 minutes. Remove and allow to cool slightly.

Serve warm with vanilla ice cream.

Sauces

In this chapter I have included sauces that would be great with seafood, meat and poultry and have given you ideas to use accordingly. I also included 6 recipes for different BBQ sauces, as these are always fun to experiment with in the warmer weather. Remember, a special sauce can elevate a dish from routine to spectacular.

Soy *and* Ginger Marinade

9	cloves **garlic**, roasted and coarsely chopped
¼	cup fresh **ginger**, grated
⅓	cup **soy sauce**
⅓	cup **cooking sherry**
⅓	cup **rice wine vinegar**
⅓	cup **olive oil**
3	tablespoons **sesame oil**

Combine all ingredients in mixing bowl.

Refrigerate until ready to use.

This is great on any kind of grilled steak.

Makes 2 cups

Yellow Tomato Salsa

4	large **yellow tomatoes**, seeded, cut into ½" pieces
3	cloves **garlic**, roasted and finely chopped
2	thick slices **grilled red onion**, finely chopped
1	**jalapeño pepper**, seeded and finely chopped
1	tablespoon **rice wine vinegar**
4	teaspoons **cilantro**, finely chopped
1	teaspoon **kosher salt**
½	teaspoon **black pepper**

Combine all ingredients in mixing bowl.

Refrigerate until ready to use.

We use this with our Lobster Quesadilla.

Makes 2 cups

Sun-Dried Tomato Relish

¼   cup **sun-dried tomatoes**, drained, finely julienned
1   small **shallot**, roasted and finely chopped
2   tablespoons **olive oil**
1   tablespoon **balsamic vinegar**
2   teaspoons **honey**
1   teaspoon **kosher salt**
½   teaspoon **black pepper**

Combine all ingredients in mixing bowl.

Refrigerate until ready to use.

This is great on crostini, grilled flatbreads, and sandwiches or with cheese. Also mix with some olives and it makes for a great appetizer.

Makes ½ cup

Red Onion Apple Relish

1   small **red onion**, sliced ¼", grilled
2   **Granny Smith apples**, peeled,
        cored and sliced ¼", grilled
2   tablespoons **white balsamic vinegar**
2   tablespoons **olive oil**
3   tablespoons **sugar**
2   teaspoons **ketchup**
      pinch **cayenne pepper**
      pinch **white pepper**

Place red onions and apples on grill and cook on both sides.

Place olive oil in saucepan and heat.

Add onions and cook until soft.

Add apples and cook until soft.

Add sugar and cook until dissolved.

Add vinegar, ketchup, cayenne pepper and white pepper. Mix well and cook until syrupy.

Remove from heat and allow to cool.

Refrigerate until ready to use.

We actually use this on a turkey sandwich but it would also be great on grilled pork chops.

Makes 1 cup

Soy Mustard Dipping Sauce

¼ cup **Dijon mustard**
¼ cup **Kikkoman Teriyaki Sauce**
½ teaspoon **black pepper**
2 teaspoons **shallots**, finely chopped
1 tablespoon **ginger**, grated
1 tablespoon fresh **lemon juice**
2 tablespoons **Wesson Oil**

Whisk Dijon mustard, Kikkoman Teriyaki sauce and black pepper together in mixing bowl.

Add shallot, ginger and lemon juice. Mix well.

Add oil slowly and whisk vigorously until emulsified.

Seared ahi tuna is the choice here.

Makes 1 cup

Key Lime Aioli

2 **egg yolks**
3 tablespoons fresh **basil**, chopped
1 tablespoon **garlic**, chopped
½ cup **olive oil**
¼ teaspoon **salt**
  pinch **white pepper**
¼ cup **key lime juice**

In a food processor combine egg yolks, basil, garlic and mix well. With machine running, slowly pour in olive oil and process until smooth.

Add salt, white pepper and key lime juice. Mix well.

Reserve until ready to use.

A good compliment to grilled fish.

Makes 1 cup

Roasted Corn-Poblano Relish

2	ears **fresh corn**, grilled
2	tablespoons **butter**, melted
1	**Poblano chili pepper**, grilled
½	**red pepper**, finely chopped
¼	cup **green onion**, thinly sliced
¼	cup **red onion**, finely chopped
2	tablespoons **cilantro**, finely chopped
1	tablespoons **lime juice**
1	tablespoon **olive oil**
1	**garlic** cloves, finely chopped
¼	cup **beefsteak tomato**, chopped into ½" pieces

Brush corn with butter and place on grill and cook on all sides until golden brown. Set aside until ready to take off cob.

Place Poblano pepper on grill and char on all sides.

Seed and chop Poblano pepper into ½" pieces.

Take corn off the cob and place in mixing bowl. Combine with all other ingredients and mix well.

Great with quesadillas or roasted chicken.

Makes 2 cups

Creole Sauce

3	tablespoons **olive oil**
1¼	cups **red onions**, julienned ½"
¾	cup **celery**, julienned ¼"
½	cup **green pepper**, julienned ½"
½	cup **red pepper**, julienned ½"
1	tablespoon **garlic**, finely chopped
1	tablespoon **File Gumbo Spice**
1	28 oz. can chopped **tomatoes**
2	cups **Lobster Stock** (see page 18)
2	teaspoons **Tabasco Sauce**
1	teaspoon **arrowroot**
2	tablespoons **water**
⅓	cup **okra**, sliced ½"

Place oil into large saucepan and heat.

Add onions and cook until golden brown.

Add celery and cook until tender.

Add peppers and garlic and cook until tender.

Sprinkle File Gumbo Spice and mix well.

Add tomatoes, Lobster Stock and Tabasco; mix well. Cook for about 30 minutes on low heat. Keep covered.

Add arrowroot/water mixture and mix well. Cook for an additional ½ hour on low heat.

Add okra, cook for 10 minutes and mix well on low heat.

We all know Creole sauce is great with shrimp or chicken, but this is also great over a Sunday omelet.

Makes 1½ quarts

Tomato-Red Pepper Salsa

1	**red beefsteak tomato**, seeded, chopped into ½" pieces
1	**yellow beefsteak tomato**, seeded, chopped into ½" pieces
1	**red pepper**, chopped into ½" pieces
2	tablespoons **green onions**, finely chopped
2	tablespoons fresh **lime juice**
1	tablespoon **olive oil**
1	tablespoon **capers**, finely chopped
2	teaspoons **cilantro**, finely chopped
½	teaspoon **salt**
¼	teaspoon **black pepper**
1	**jalapeño pepper**, seeded, finely chopped
1	**garlic** clove, finely chopped

Combine all ingredients in mixing bowl.

Refrigerate until ready to use.

Makes 2 cups

Hawaiian Marinade

½	cup **soy sauce**
½	cup **pineapple juice**
¼	cup **sesame oil**
½	cup **rice wine vinegar**
1	tablespoon **ginger**, grated
2	teaspoons **garlic**, finely chopped
2	tablespoons **brown sugar**

Combine all ingredients in mixing bowl.

Refrigerate until ready to use.

Great with tuna, salmon or swordfish.

Makes 2 cups

The Grill's BBQ Sauce

3	cups	**Original Open Pit BBQ Sauce**
1	cup	**ketchup**
½	cup	**bourbon**
¼	cup	**orange juice**
¼	cup	**maple syrup**
2	teaspoons	**Lea & Perrins**
1	teaspoon	**salt**
½	teaspoon	**black pepper**

Place Open Pit BBQ Sauce into large mixing bowl.

Add remainder of the ingredients and mix thoroughly.

Refrigerate until ready to use.

This is what we have used as our base BBQ sauce for years.

Makes 1 quart

Kahlua-Espresso BBQ Sauce

2	tablespoons	**extra virgin olive oil**
2	tablespoons	**garlic**, finely chopped
¼	cup	**Kahlua liquor**
1	cup	**ketchup**
1	cup	**honey**
½	cup	**balsamic vinegar**
¼	cup	**soy sauce**
¼	cup	**brewed espresso**
1	tablespoon	**Lea & Perrins**
½	teaspoon	**kosher salt**
½	teaspoon	**ancho chili powder**

Heat oil in saucepan over low heat and sauté garlic until golden.

Add all ingredients and cook on medium heat until reduced by ¼, about 30–45 minutes.

Refrigerate until ready to use.

Try this on roasted duck.

Makes 2 cups

Zinfandel Chile Jam BBQ Sauce

3	tablespoons	**olive oil**
½	cup	**Spanish onion**, finely chopped
⅓	cup	**ancho chili powder**
1	teaspoon	**cumin**
2		**garlic** cloves, finely chopped
1½	cups	**Red Zinfandel Wine**
1½	cups	**water**
⅔	cup	**balsamic vinegar**
⅔	cup	**black currant preserves**
½	cup	**brown sugar**
2	tablespoons	**tomato paste**
⅓	cup	**The Grill's BBQ Sauce** (see page 185)
1	teaspoon	**kosher salt**
½	teaspoon	**black pepper**

Heat oil in saucepan. Add onion and cook until golden.

Add chili powder, cumin, garlic and cook over low heat until lightly browned.

Add the wine and cook over low heat until mixture is thick, about 15 minutes.

Add water, vinegar, preserves, brown sugar, tomato paste, The Grill's BBQ Sauce, salt and pepper and cook over medium heat until reduced by ¼, about 50–60 minutes. Allow to cool.

Purée in blender. Refrigerate until ready to use.

Finger-licking good. Great on chicken, duck or pork!

Makes 1 quart

Mango BBQ Sauce

2		large **red tomatoes**, grilled and coarsely chopped
1		**green pepper**, grilled and coarsely chopped
1		**red pepper**, grilled and coarsely chopped
1		**mango**, peeled, pitted and coarsely chopped
½	cup	**water**
⅓	cup	**red onions**, chopped
⅓	cup	**brown sugar**
⅓	cup	**cider vinegar**
2	tablespoons	**molasses**
2	tablespoons	**Dijon mustard**
1	tablespoon	**cinnamon**
1	tablespoon	**garlic**, chopped
1	teaspoon	**ground cumin**
1	teaspoon	fresh **thyme**, chopped
1	teaspoon	fresh **basil**, chopped
1		**jalapeño chili pepper**, halved

Combine all ingredients in large saucepot and bring to a boil.

Reduce heat and simmer for 30 minutes. Allow to cool.

Purée in food processor and refrigerate until ready to use.

Try this on grilled shrimp or scallops.

Makes 2 cups

Moroccan BBQ Sauce

½	cup **honey**
¼	cup **rice wine vinegar**
1	tablespoon **soy sauce**
¼	cup **ketchup**
½	**cinnamon stick**
1	star **anise**
½	teaspoon **Chinese chili paste**
¼	teaspoon **cardamom**
½	teaspoon **coriander seed**
½	teaspoon **ginger**, grated
¼	teaspoon whole **cloves**
½	teaspoon **black peppercorns**
2	tablespoons **cilantro**, chopped
1	tablespoon fresh **lime juice**

Combine all ingredients in a saucepan.

Bring to a boil and cook over medium/low heat for 30 minutes or reduced by ½.

Strain. Refrigerate until ready to use.

Excellent on grilled chicken or game birds.

Makes 2 cups

Pork Loin BBQ Sauce

1	cup **ketchup**
1	**jalapeño pepper**, seeded, finely chopped
¼	cup **cider vinegar**
1	tablespoon **Lea & Perrins**
2	tablespoons chopped **garlic**
1	tablespoon fresh **lime juice**
¼	cup **brown sugar**
⅓	cup **olive oil**
1	teaspoon **ground coriander**
1	teaspoon **kosher salt**
1	teaspoon **ginger**, grated
¼	cup **honey**
¼	cup **red onions**, finely chopped

Bring all ingredients to a boil in a large saucepan.

Allow to cool, then purée in a blender. Refrigerate until ready to use.

Fantastic on a roasted pork rack.

Makes 2 cups

Pecan-Lemon Butter

2	sticks **butter**, softened
2	tablespoons **pecan halves**, toasted and chopped
2	tablespoons fresh **parsley**, chopped
1	tablespoon fresh **lemon juice**

Whip butter in mixer.

Add all ingredients and mix well.

Refrigerate until ready to use.

This is excellent with sole or a roasted Atlantic cod.

Makes ½ cup

Green Chili Pesto

2	**garlic** cloves
⅓	cup **Parmesan cheese**, freshly grated
2	**Poblano chili peppers**, roasted, peeled and seeded
½	cup **pine nuts**
4	tablespoons fresh **parsley**, chopped
2	tablespoons **cilantro**, chopped
4	tablespoons **olive oil**

Place all ingredients in food processor and mix well.

Refrigerate until ready to use.

This is fantastic on grilled catfish.

Makes 1 cup

Peach Chutney

1	cup **white wine vinegar**
⅓	cup **brown sugar**
½	cup **peach nectar**
1	teaspoon **salt**
½	teaspoon **ground cloves**
1	tablespoon **ginger**, grated
½	teaspoon **ground cinnamon**
2	tablespoons **jalapeño peppers**, finely chopped and seeded
3	tablespoons **dried cherries**
⅓	cup **dried cranberries**
1½	cups **peaches**, peeled, chopped into ½" piece
½	cup **pears**, peeled, chopped into ½" pieces

Place all ingredients except fruits into a saucepan. Heat to boiling. Reduce heat and simmer uncovered for 20 minutes.

Add dried cherries, cook for 10 minutes.

Add dried cranberries, cook for 5 minutes.

Add peaches and pears; cook until slightly thickened. Keep warm.

This is fantastic on pork tenderloin, grilled chicken or even on Thanksgiving Day for a great compliment to roasted turkey.

Makes 2 cups

Olive Oil Vegetable Garlic Sauce

4	cloves **garlic**
2	cups **olive oil**
4	tablespoons **Vegetable Base** (see sources, page 192)
1	cup hot **water**
1	tablespoon fresh **chives**, finely chopped
2	teaspoons **sun-dried tomatoes**

Place 1 cup of the olive oil into blender cup and add garlic, blend until garlic is emulsified.

Mix Vegetable Base with ½ cup of hot water, and completely dissolve.

Place remaining olive oil into saucepot and heat.

Add garlic and oil mixture to hot oil and take off stove immediately, mix in well.

Add the chives and mix well.

Add the Vegetable Base mixture, sun-dried tomatoes and the remaining ½ cup of hot water.

Whip entire mixture well. Refrigerate until ready to use.

Makes 4 cups

Basil Aioli

2	**egg yolks**
1	**garlic** clove, finely chopped
½	teaspoon fresh **lemon juice**
¼	teaspoon **Dijon mustard**
	pinch **cayenne pepper**
½	cup **olive oil**
¼	cup **heavy cream**
3	tablespoons fresh **basil**, finely chopped
1	tablespoon **butter**, melted

Place egg yolks, garlic, lemon juice, Dijon mustard, cayenne pepper in food processor and blend well.

Add olive oil slowly until well blended.

Add cream, basil and butter and mix very well.

Makes 1 cup

Sources

Earthly Delights
4180 Keller Road
Suite B
Holt, MI 48842
Specialty produce, mushrooms, & herbs

Previn Inc.
2044 Rittenhouse Square
Philadelphia, PA 19103
(215) 985-1996
www.previninc.com
Specialty cookware and bakeware

J.B. Prince
36 East 31st Street
New York, NY 10016
(212) 683-3553
www.jbprince.com
Specialty cookware

Zingerman's
422 Detroit Street
Ann Arbor, MI 48104
(888) 636-8162
www.zingermans.com
Specialty sausages, cheeses, Tasso ham,
Chorizo sausage, pomegranate molasses and olive oils

King Arthur Flour Co.
The Baker's Catalogue
P.O. Box 876
Nolwich, VT 05055
(800) 827-6836
www.kingarthurflour.com
Sea salt, vanilla beans, nut powders

The Chef's Garden
9009 Huron Avery Road
Huron, OH 44839
(800) 289-4644
Specialty produce

Penzey's Spice House
P.O. Box 1448
Waukesha, WI 53187
(414) 574-0277
(800) 741-7787
www.penzeys.com
Assorted Spices

www.ethnicgrocers.com
Specialty ethnic foods, Chinese Chile Paste,
Hoisin sauce, Masa flour, pomegranate molasses

All Serve, Inc.
P.O. Box 21743
Cleveland, OH 44121
(800) 827-8328
www.soupbase.com
Seafood Base
Vegetable Base
Lobster Base

Al Dente Pasta Co.
9815 Main Street
Northfield Township, MI 48180
(734) 449-8522
(800) 536-7278
www.aldentepasta.com
Assorted pastas and pasta sauces

Index